The Entertaining Cat Lovers Guide

How to Understand Your Cat

Funny Feline and Cat Lover Facts and Valuable Insights that Strengthen Your Bond with Your Cat

D1522792

Julie Dirks

Cover Design
Michael H. LaChapelle

For all the cats I've loved

Kitty, Topaz and Amber, Spats, Smidgling, Tar,
Ham and Cesil

Table of Contents

Introduction

Who are cats, these essentially wild little beasties, and how did they become the house cats we know today? Why are cats so mysterious and unknowable when there is so much history about them from ancient Egypt to the present? What is it about the pussy cat that cat lovers can't resist? In gaining an understanding of these glorious creatures' history and makeup, it becomes clearer why we are so attracted to them. While their unique anatomy lends itself to humor, it also gives them an aura of otherworldliness, magic. No other being shares many of the traits of the feline. The fascinating anatomy that is the domestic cat is more unique than you think.

But what do cats think about us? What do they like? They make it quite clear what they don't like usually but there are things cat parents can do to minimize the "don't likes". How can we make our cats' lives as well as our own as fun, rich, loving, and satisfying as possible?

After a glorious lifetime of living with cats, the observations, experiences, research, and humorous conjecture build a fascinating profile of our mini-lions and some insights into our pussy cats that can be both amusing and used to enhance your life with cats. Forewarning: As much of this is personal experience-based, the cat representation draws from the medium and long-haired varieties that populated my life but ninety-nine percent is applicable to all types. This is not a breed-specific book but rather it takes a look at domestic cats that bide in our home, how and why that came to be, both scientifically and humorously.

The Fabulous Folks that

Adore Our Feline Friends

One small cat changes coming home to an empty house to coming home.–Pam Brown

The personalities of cat owners often reflect those of their feline companions. Not that they are double-jointed acrobats, hunters, or divas, but cats tend to be reserved, highly observant creatures, naturally solitary (does not mean cannot become quite social), and their owners tend to be the same. Cats seem to be just the right pet for those of us who are more introverted and sensitive. Cat lovers are often portrayed as crazy cat zealots, which is false. Okay, mostly false. You do have to be a teensy bit of a high-risk taker to cohabit with an animal that sometimes shows its affection with claws, fangs, a sandpaper-rough tongue, and the occasional gift of a disemboweled bird on your pillow.

A 2017 study by three U.S. psychologists on cat people and dog people provided some interesting insights regarding what makes a cat person. It seems that cat people scored higher on general intelligence tests and abstract thought and reasoning, which suggests you have to be pretty smart when dealing with these mysterious and sometimes obstinate creatures.

The study also found that cat people have a tendency to be shy, freethinking, serious, and sentimental folks, as opposed to their dog-loving counterparts who tend to be more outgoing, pragmatic, dutiful, and sociable. This is by no means a rule. Cats don't follow most rules anyway.

There is also more than a little creativity, self-reliance, open-mindedness, and a tendency to be defiant in cat lovers. A lot of artists, activists, writers, and creators own cats, many even finding inspiration from their feline muses, for instance: legendary painters Gustav Klimt and Henri Matisse, animal rights activists and actresses Betty White and Hannah Shaw, also known as Kitten Lady, famed authors Stephen King and Jirō Osaragi, and visionary creators Andy Warhol and Salvador Dalí. The quirks of cat lovers, much like their cats, possibly stem from their open-minded, free-spirited view of the world along with their cat ownership. Because cat people are so independent, they value the affection their cats can provide as much as their companionship.

More city dwellers are cat owners, which could mean that the pressure of city living gets to them and that the comforting rumble from their favorite purr monster is just what they need to drain the stress of the day away.

Cats also adapt to living in cramped spaces and are fairly easy to keep indoors, likely due to their history of being bred in small living quarters in ancient Egyptian catteries. They are inquisitive little escape artists though.

The Numbers Speak for Themselves

There are approximately 600 million cats in the world, according to the World Atlas (Price, 2023). An estimated 62.2% or approximately 373 million of the total cat population are kept as pets.

In the United States: Despite the old cat lady misconception, the Millennial generation makes up 33% of cat ownership, with Generation Z catching up with 25% ownership of the estimated total of 60.2–61.9 million pet cats in the U.S. as of 2022 according to Megna (2023).

Cat celebrities like Grumpy Cat, Smudge the Cat, and Lil Bub have certainly done their due diligence by sensationalizing cats on the internet and in popular media. The percentage of Zoomers owning cats is steadily growing. The last few decades have seen an overall increase in the popularity of our feline friends. Twenty-nine percent of U.S. households own cats, that's about 46.5 million of them. (Megna, 2023).

The total number of feral cats, however, well exceeds the pet cat population, with an estimated 100 million cats, making the U.S. the country with the largest total cat population in the world! They should have a state of their own and call it Wiscatson, or Vermeownt, seeing as their near-namesakes have some of the largest cat populations in the U.S. The feral population produces 80% of the total kittens born making cat adoption a blessing rather than buying one from a breeder. Trap Neuter Return programs are in place and have reduced their population by 66% in the last decade (Nolen, 2017).

A cat lovers publication, The Purring Journal (2022), provides some interesting feline statistics from countries around the world, such as the following locations.

- Germany has an estimated pet cat population of 16.7 million as of 2021, and an estimated 1 million feral cats. Of the 41.6 million German households, 26% of them have cats.

- France has a pet cat population of around 15.1 million but has a staggering feral cat population in comparison, estimated to be 13 million plus. France holds the record for being the country with the highest abandonment rates, with 100,000 cats being abandoned every summer.

- The United Kingdom has an estimated 12 million pet cats with an estimated 250,000 feral cats. Each of the 8 million households, that's 28% of UK households, has an average of 1.5 resident fluffballs. The cat population has tripled over the last sixty years.

Paws-itively Purrrfect Cat

Components

Cat anatomy and physiology are fascinating and so unique that they deserve their own chapter.

The Fur

Fur is doubtless one of the best features of a cat, though people with allergies might not agree. For those people, there are a few hairless breeds that can accommodate. The secret is that it's not actually the fur they are allergic to, but more on that later. Whether fur is long or short, the feeling of running your fingers through its softness is unanimously enjoyable for cats and humans alike.

There is a lot of fur on a cat, as many as 130,000 hairs per square inch of skin. Each cat possesses several types of fur that serve different functions:

- Primary hairs, also known as guard hairs, are coarse hairs that taper to a finer tip. They insulate the cat, protect its skin, help repel water, and serve as tactile input, similar to but not as good as whiskers. They also determine the color of a cat's coat.

- Awn hairs, also called the base coat, are sometimes the same length as guard hairs, but are more often shorter and finer.

- The undercoat, also called down, are the thin hairs that grow closest to the skin. Their soft fluffiness provides another layer of insulation to keep cats warm. Their "undies" are also prone to twisting in a knot and may tangle and mat if Kitty isn't a great groomer.

Outdoor cats shed seasonally during spring and fall, while indoor cats shed all the time. Some cat owners affectionately call the shed fur pet glitter, especially when it's pointed out to them by others in public. They might also have simply given up on the never-ending battle of fur removal.

There are fewer long-haired cats than short ones because it is a recessive, genetic trait that both parents must pass on to their offspring. If only one parent contributes the short hair gene, being dominant, the kitten will be short-haired. There are exceptions to the rule, but it requires a few more technical genetic mechanisms explained.

The color of a cat's fur is also decided by genetics, but some genes may interfere with other genes. For example, when the white spotting gene cancels out a fur color it makes a bicolor cat, like the black and white Tuxedo. Maltese or gray cats have a dominant gene that normally prevents reddish fur. The genes for red fur and black fur are on separate X chromosomes. This is why calico or tortoiseshell cats are practically all females since they will have both of the X chromosomes. Calico or tortoiseshell males are sterile anomalies since males should have only one X chromosome and one Y chromosome. The agouti gene that is responsible for the tabby pattern needs only one parent with the gene to produce a tabby pattern in 50% of their kittens. That is why most cats have the tabby pattern, even if tabbies come in a rainbow of colors.

Color-pointed fur protects the most exposed parts, like the ears, faces, feet, tail, and male genitalia of light-colored cats from the sun. It is believed to be an adaptation to warmer climates.

Many people think that cat hair causes allergies, but this is not true. The truth is somewhat more, um, hard to swallow. The allergies people experience are caused by a protein in cat saliva. When cats groom themselves, which they do almost as often as sleeping, they coat their fur with a thin layer of saliva that flakes off when it dries. These tiny flakes are called dander and it's literally everywhere. Cats with longer hair will produce more dander, which gives rise to the misconception that it's the hair that causes the allergy and it might have contributed to the debunked myth that cat breath causes consumption. The good news is that dander can be controlled by thorough house cleaning. Also, special hypo-allergenic cats have been bred to eliminate allergic reactions people might have to dander, and they are not all hairless breeds. Now even more people can enjoy the magic of cat ownership.

The Head

The Eyes

The eyes are the mirrors of the soul, they say, and you can tell a lot by looking into a cat's eyes. They might even bless you with a heart-melting slow blink, reserved for only the most trusted of humans. By blinking slowly cats communicate trust and that they have let their guard down. The fun part is that it's a universal gesture every cat understands, so when you make friends with your neighborhood cats you can blink slowly for them too. It's the polite thing to do.

So, why do cats have big, shiny alien eyes?

A biologically reflective layer of tissue inside the eyes called the tapetum lucidum reflects available light internally for another go at the retina, allowing cats to see in light six times dimmer than we can. It also gives them that glittery shine when they lurk in the shadows, making them perfect for 3 a.m. rampages around the house.

Cats have trouble focusing on things closer to them than 12 inches and rely more on their whiskers when things get up close and personal. That's because of their large eyes, which are better suited to seeing threats, prey, and treats from further away. Their eyes have highly adaptive pupils that can contract or dilate at the drop of a mouse thanks to two additional muscles per eye. As lowly humans, we can only dilate our pupils 15 times larger than their minimum aperture, but cats can dilate their pupils to an astounding 135 times their minimum to allow more light to enter their eyes.

The vertical pupils of the domestic cat have likely evolved due to hunting and being low to the ground where there's more grass and obstacles obstructing their view. The vertical-slit pupils give them better depth perception and let them see vertical contours more sharply. Their brain then analyzes the slight differences in the information received from each eye. This gives them great accuracy when pouncing on prey or toys and also makes those impossible jumps possible, most of the time.

What do cats see on TV? According to the cat food maker Hills, on their Hillspet.com website, "Because of the structure of their eyes, cats are more likely to engage in television that contains a combination of red, green and blue paired with swiftly moving objects." As personally observed by the Beat Generation writer, William S. Burroughs, without the benefit of the Hills research, "Cat videos may be all the rage among humans, but cats prefer the avian versions." Hills might add red, green, and blue *birds* preferred.

Lastly, in addition to their normal eyelids, cats also have a third eyelid called the nictitating membrane underneath the other two which can partially cover the eye to protect the cornea from scratches and prickly grass. This membrane also covers a cat's eyes during deep sleep but retracts quickly when it wakes up. A cat coming out of anesthesia will always have the nictitating membrane lowered over the eye which looks quite disturbing as it is a solid white color where the cat's lovely eye usually appears.

The Ears

One of a cat's most distinctive features is its large triangular ears, with hair inside and out. The wispy inside hairs are called ear furnishings and come in a variety of different lengths, with some sticking out quite far from the ear flaps, but they ultimately serve the same purpose. They keep out dirt and enhance a cat's hearing by channeling even the slightest noise into the inner ear. A form of kitty radar.

Some cats have distinctive ear tufts or lynx tips sticking up on the tips of their ears, giving them a much wilder look. The most remarkable ear tufts belong to the Maine Coon, and are second only to the Lynx.

Cat ears have an impressive 32 muscles that give them 180° of rotation (Bukowski, 2018), so they can swivel around like radar dishes and pinpoint exactly where a noise came from, and if it's you, decide to ignore you or not.

Cat's ears sport another trick: Henry's pockets, otherwise known as a cutaneous marginal pouch. It's the tiny fold of skin that forms a small hollow on the lower part near the base of the outer ear. It's a mystery why cats have Henry's pockets. All we know is that they can sometimes harbor harvest mites. Eeewww! There are some theories that Henry's pockets pick up high-frequency sounds or that they aid ear rotation when it is flattened.

A cat's inner ear houses an impressive vestibular system, which is like a compass, telling them which way is up or down with great accuracy, even while they are tumbling in midair. It also gives cats superior balance, making those stomach-churning tightrope walks they do a breeze.

Within the ear are incredibly sensitive cochlea, the hearing organ. They can hear faint sounds and frequencies much higher or lower than we can, even better than most dogs, which makes not hearing us obviously a choice.

The Nose

That damp little button surrounding a cat's nostrils is called its nose leather. If you were to try and take a nose print from two different cats, and you're successful in escaping both times with your skin intact, you'll find that no two nose leathers are alike. They are the cat version of fingerprints.

The color of their nose leather is typically related to the color of their fur. Black cats have black noses and white cats have pink noses, while some tabbies have multicolored or freckled noses. Sometimes when your cat is excited or hot you might notice it turning a darker shade as more blood flushes its nose leather. Like a nose blush.

The nose leather is an extension of a cat's olfactory system and can detect humidity and temperature up close and gauge the direction in which the wind is blowing. You'll often see cats licking their nose leathers, perhaps to make checking the direction of the wind easier like humans who lick a finger and hold it up. Or it might be to clean off a lingering tuna scent that's throwing off their sniffer. Since cats have a poor sense of taste, it might make food smell better and stimulate their appetite, but it's really just another mystery only cats know the answer to.

The Whiskers

A cat's whiskers, also known as vibrissae, are super-sensitive with a range of functions. Cats use their whiskers to navigate in the dark, as we do with our toes and outstretched arms, albeit with more grace and less cursing. Their whisker length is in proportion to the width of their body, so they know that if their head (whiskers and all) fits through a hole, their body is sure to follow. In 2005, the world record for longest whiskers went to a Maine Coon from Finland called Fullmoon's Miss American Pie, or Missi to her friends, and measured a whopping 7.5 inches (Breyer, 2023). Missi's weight remains undisclosed to preserve her dignity.

A cat's whiskers are two to three times thicker than its other hairs and have roots going three times deeper into the skin to connect to the nervous system via proprioceptors. The slightest stimulation of these receptors can tell a cat anything from the relative position of its head to its body, to the location of its noisiest toy in complete darkness, though it fails to detect food in half-filled bowls.

Avoid touching your cat's whiskers, because just like you, cats are also sensitive to having the obvious pointed out and prodded at. Whisker stress occurs when cats' whiskers are overstimulated. Give that fussy eater a wider bowl so its whiskers don't touch and it might turn out whisker stress was the issue if they are not eating or drinking.

A cat's whiskers not only adorn its cheeks, as is the case with the mythic-sized whiskers, but are also found on the chin (mandibular whiskers), antennae-like eyebrows (superciliary whiskers), on the back of the legs (carpal whiskers), and by the ears, which are simply called ear-tufts.

Though they look like eyebrows to us, a cat's eye whiskers trigger a protective reflex more like our eyelashes do when encountering dust or other potential hazards. The combination of mouth whiskers, antennae whiskers, and ear whiskers sticking out all over their heads like a bug seem incongruous and yet altogether they make a great contribution to the feline faces we adore.

While we may have issues with hair sprouting in awkward places, whiskers provide essential tactile input for cats. They can feel the slightest twitch and even detect the heartbeat of their prey. Whiskers pick up vibrations from touch or from the movement of the air around them. It helps cats pinpoint nearby prey as their eyesight up close is so poor.

The position of a cat's whiskers also signals some of its emotional states. Sideways-pointing whiskers indicate calm contentedness, whiskers directed forward indicate curiosity and vigilance, but whiskers pulled back against the cheeks indicate that someone is about to regret some recent decisions.

Whiskers don't shed often, and excessive whisker loss should be looked at by a vet, but the occasional loss of one or two is no cause for alarm. Just make a wish and blow it away.

The Mouth

Tongue. Ah, to be blessed by a lick from your furry friend. We've likely all felt the roughness of it before, especially after the first few licks, but why is it so rough?

A cat's tongue is covered with hundreds of tiny backward-facing keratin spines called *filiform papillae*. If keratin sounds familiar, it's because it's the same substance hair and nails are made of, so a tongue with tiny claws is closer to the truth. All felids have barbed tongues. So, why exactly do they need a tongue like that? There are a few reasons:

- The barbs on their tongue shred meat, can scrape the meat off bones, and help to move food to the back of their mouth. It's especially useful in the wild when food is harder to come by and every tiny bit counts.

- They are perfect for grooming. Their mouths have a full-on salon installed, but it's not all about getting clean and looking stylish. The many filiform papillae are perfect for grooming. The inner curve of these tiny spines is concave along its length, like scoops, so they can scrape dead skin, loose hair, and debris up from the roots while also detangling the fur, but wait, there's more! With each lick, the scoops simultaneously apply saliva like a shampoo to help clean those sticky or greasy spots and distribute the natural oils from the cat's skin all over their fur, adding a nice water-resistant gloss.

- They apply saliva to their bodies to help cool them down in warm weather.

- The way a cat drinks water is out of this world. It uses the tip of its spiny tongue to lightly touch the water's surface, then quickly retract it. This causes the water to be drawn up in a column toward their mouths, but before the column can break, they chomp down on it. All this happens at a rate of about four times per second and requires expert timing: if they lap too fast the water column breaks too early and if they lap too slowly the water doesn't form a column. The cat swallows every few laps before the water can run back out.

Interestingly, cats are the only mammals who can't taste sweetness. They lack a specific gene that tells the brain something is sweet, and they either perceive sweet as something else entirely, or not at all. A cat's ability to taste sugar likely didn't evolve because they are obligate carnivores who had no need to develop a taste for carbohydrates. Additionally, they don't have glucokinase enzymes which are found in the liver that help with the digestion of carbs and control glucose levels. If only we humans could avoid the sweet stuff quite as easily. However, cats have a taste receptor that we don't. Cats can taste adenosine triphosphate (ATP), the energy carrier of all living cells that helps cats track down prey.

You might notice your cat's tongue sticking out on occasion. It's not blowing raspberries, it might just be taking a break from grooming itself or, if its mouth is open as well, and it has a far-off look in its eyes it might have just smelled something that needs further analysis. This expression is called the flehmen reaction, colloquially known as stink face. Cats possess a Jacobson's organ or vomeronasal organ on the roof of their mouths. This specialized organ connects the mouth and nose through ducts and analyzes airborne pheromones from other cats, mostly those found in their pee. Having a flehmen reaction right about now?

Teeth. As a predator, cats have an impressive maw. We usually only get to see the tips of their fangs sticking out when they meow, but when they yawn it becomes quite clear that you don't want to get on the wrong side of a cat. Their awesome fangs come in handy for hunting, grooming, and defense, or the occasional reminder that they've had enough petting.

Kittens have more baby teeth than humans start out with. The 26 tiny milk teeth come out when kittens are 2 weeks old and fall out by 3 months to make space for their 30 permanent teeth.

The two rows of six tiny incisors each, situated right in front of a cat's mouth are useful for gripping or nibbling objects and grooming themselves. They look like baby teeth but aren't. They aren't very useful for hunting, but their four canines certainly are.

Their sharp canines or fangs are what puncture the skin and deliver the killing bite, but every coin has two sides, and the other side of killer teeth is that they also function as a four-pronged comb, great for grooming when they need to remove extra tough tangles. After all, every cat is a glamor puss.

Last but not least are a cat's serrated premolars and molars. They work a bit like steak knives as they shear flesh and connective tissue off of bones. You'll notice them in action when your mini-lion tackles a particularly tough or large piece of meat and bites it with the sides of its jaws (they may even growl if approached). They don't really chew much once the meat is in their mouths, and often simply swallow the sheared-off bits. Swallowing without chewing comes in handy when our domestic cats lose some or all of their permanent teeth. Cats will eat most of their food with minimal chewing and will often gulp their dry food down without any issues. Best to stick with soft wet food for old toothless though.

Cats do suffer from the same dental issues as we do, with a few exceptions:

- They don't get cavities. Unlike our teeth, a cat's teeth don't have horizontal surfaces where cavity-causing bacteria thrive. They're not big on eating sugar either.

- Cats rarely display signs of dental issues, so it's up to us to observe them closely. If their eating habits suddenly change, they lose a tooth (adults shouldn't be losing teeth), or their breath becomes bad, it might be time to visit a vet. You can have a look yourself, if allowed, for anything out of the ordinary, but it is best to let a professional have a look.

- Cats over the age of four have abysmally bad teeth; 50%–90% of them have dental problems and are especially susceptible to feline tooth resorption, gingivitis, periodontal disease, and stomatitis.

Most of these dental issues can be prevented with regular dental care and annual dental check-ups. It's recommended that their teeth should be cleaned by age four and then every two to three years but it depends on the cat. While a cat can still survive with some missing or bad teeth, it can shorten and make for a less enjoyable life. There are trusted and effective dental products for cats on the market bearing the Veterinary Oral Health Council's seal.

Brush your cat's teeth, if you can, but with special pet toothpaste and not with human toothpaste. Cats not used to having their teeth brushed will have a hard time getting used to it, so it's best to form the habit while they are kittens. There are other options for those stubborn felines who refuse to have their teeth brushed, like specially formulated water additives, kibble, and treats that can reduce plaque and fix the tuna breath.

The Voice

Cats speak only to those who know how to listen. –Sigmund Freud

Purring. Up until recently, we have been in the dark about how cats make the purring sound, and it turns out that some other animals purr, too. Some of these animals are somewhat similar to cats, like genets which are more closely related to mongooses than to cats, and some are decidedly un-catlike, like hyenas, tapirs, guinea pigs, raccoons, and even gorillas, though the latter does it only while they feed. Only members of the cat family and the civet family, like the aforementioned genet, are capable of a true purr though, the other animals are simply copycats.

A true purr starts in the central nervous system (CNS) with a neural oscillator, more commonly known as brainwaves. This rhythmic activity in the CNS is a response triggered by some stimuli and sends a signal to the muscles in your cat's larynx (the voice box). These muscles then start to vibrate between 25–140 times per second, making that distinctive rumble both while inhaling and exhaling.

The world is a dark and unfamiliar place for a newborn kitten, especially for the first 10-12 days as their eyes have not opened yet, so it's good to know that mom is nearby. Their mother's purr is the most familiar and comforting thing they know and the sound helps guide her blind litter toward her. Kittens purr instinctively, and the back-and-forth purring reassures each one of the other's presence. It's like a rhythmic lullaby.

A cat will usually purr when it is relaxed and content, but they are known to purr when they feel nervous, or even when they are in pain. In most cases though it's a good sign. The clever little critters will even use it to get us to do something for them. Their very infantile mewling and purring, called solicitation purrs, triggers our built-in need to nurture. Ever noticed them rubbing up against your legs with a purr and a meow? It's hard to say no to them and they know it.

Another very interesting theory sounds like it's straight out of a fantasy novel. Healing vibes! When cats purr at the low frequency of 25 Hz (25 cycles per second), it calms them down by releasing endorphins when they are stressed (Purina, 2022).

A new hypothesis is that purring at 26 Hz sends tremors through their bodies that help them recover faster from injuries, mends bones, and tendons, reduces inflammation and pain, and stimulates their muscles. It is similar to the effects vibrational therapy has on tissue regeneration in human subjects.

What is even more fantastic is that there's evidence that their purrs can possibly do the same for us. The results of a 2009 study by Adnan Qureshi, MD, et al., show that cat owners have a significantly lower risk of dying from heart attacks, heart disease, and strokes. Their purrs might also help mend our bones, reduce osteoporosis risks, reduce blood pressure, and ease migraines, to name but a few of the miracles cats can perform.

Despite all of the research that's been done on the soothing rumble of their little engines, the purring process is still shrouded in mystery.

Hissing. Hissing is typically a defensive behavior that cats and several other animals including snakes, geese, and even cockroaches use to communicate fear, frustration, or displeasure. The hissing sound is created by forcefully expelling air through the mouth or nostrils. With cats, the "hiss" sound comes through the mouth and is sometimes combined with other body signals such as the Halloween arched back with standing fur, flattened ears, and dilated pupils.

However, hissing can also be an inter-cat communication. A mother cat can hiss at her kittens to warn them away from danger or to teach behavior lessons. Cats can also hiss when they are feeling uncomfortable or overstimulated as in too much or too rough play.

Meowing. There have been extensive studies into cat meowing, too much to cover here in more than a summary. Meowing has developed in large part in response to humans talking to their fur babies. A very basic meow is used by mother cats occasionally and the caterwaul is exclusively limited to mating but for the most part, other meow vocalizations are used with humans exclusively.

New York psychologist, Mildred Moelk, also a cat lover, categorized 16 sounds used in cat-human and cat-cat communication. "Vocalizing In the House Cat: A Phonetic And Functional Study" appeared in 1944 in *Journal of Comparative Psychology*, and she organized cat vocals into three major patterns based on mouth open, closed, or open to closed: The three patterns' expressions are:

- Soft murmurs or consonants made with the mouth closed are a greeting, acknowledgment or satisfaction

- Examples are "hello," "ok" and purring =a human long, deep sigh

- Vowel sounds from an open-to-closing mouth as in meowing are requests or complaints

- Examples are "pay attention to me," "give me," "please give me," "don't" "I'm warning you"

- Loud sounds called strained intensity patterns, emitted from a wide-open mouth are arousal or stress signals

- Examples are a growl and snarl meaning "I REALLY don't like what's going on", a shrill scream is "ouch" like when a paw or tail is stepped on, a refusal is a raspy sound, spitting is one step away from attack and the uniquely feline caterwauling occurs during arousal and mating

Although emphasizing that their sounds are not words, Moelk said cats routinely change the duration, intensity, tone, pitch, roughness, stress, speed, and repetitions to communicate their goals and desires. Sounds much like humans.

Seventy years later, experts agree that cats are communicating something to us, although what is still unclear. The most widely-held theory currently, developed over a decade ago by Michael J. Owren, Ph.D., is that cats use vocalization to influence or manipulate humans, not to deliver specific information.

"Cats produce meows to get attention and rely on the owner to infer what the cat wants," explained Owren, a psychologist and professor who studied animal vocalizations until his death in January 2014.

"A person can pretty readily figure out what's going on from the cat's body posture—whether staring or other behaviors—so the cat doesn't need to have a particular acoustic meow" for each situation, Owren said. "This is communication because it is using a non-linguistic signal to affect the behavior of others. The human response gets the cat what it's seeking," although it's unknown whether the cat plans for specific reactions.

Cats succeed with their vocalizations, whether the sounds are pleasant or unpleasant, Owren added. When cats purr, "which is very appealing to humans, [cats] want the humans to continue doing whatever they're doing. When cats get excited, their loud meows are so annoying that people will do whatever they think the cat wants," just to stop the noise. Pretty smart.

The Body Beautiful

Spine and Flexibility

Cats have a unique skeleton that makes them amazingly flexible, so much so that they blur the lines between solid and liquid. Well, not really, but they do fit the bill when it comes to taking the shape of the container they are in, and in the graceful flow with which they move.

Their flexibility gives cats the upper hand when squeezing into tight spaces, and is due in part to them having a free-floating rudimentary collarbone or clavicle that's deeply nestled in their shoulder muscles. It's not connected to the other bones in their body via ligaments or joints but by muscle alone. This allows a cat's shoulder blades to move independently, granting them a greater range of motion and extending their running strides.

A cat's spine takes the bulk of the credit for giving them superior flexibility. Their slinky spines have 30 vertebrae, six more than we do in adulthood, with an elastic cushioning disc between each which allows them to twist and turn their bodies up to 180° with ease, meaning that their front legs and back legs face in the complete opposite direction (Richards, 2023). A twist of more than 90° would normally break a human's back. The muscles connected to their spines extend their running strides even further than what their loose shoulders already allow, giving their backs that graceful undulation when they run.

Though cats don't technically always land on their feet, they can effortlessly right themselves in the air with a quick reflex, using their flexible spines, special collarbones, and vestibular systems in concert.

Cats will often contort themselves into the weirdest positions when they groom themselves, creating some of the best photo ops. Their flexible spines make those hard-to-reach places easier to clean. They will sometimes even roll into very unnatural positions when they sleep but never fear, they are quite comfortable that way. We'll choose to overlook this fact when thinking about their feline grace.

Cat Sleep Poses

You can't look at a sleeping cat and be tense. –Jane Pauley

The place and position of our furry partners in sleep can tell us a lot about the headspace they are in.

The Crescent: Curled in a c-shape, the tail wrapped around instinctually protects the chest and belly, and also conserves body heat. The crescent, often used for sleeping in a box or other enclosed space, can mean that they are seeking out a secure place to rest in. They are possibly feeling unsafe, but it could very well just be the novelty of the thing. Observe their waking behavior if you have concerns.

Sleeping and peeping, or sleeping with half-lidded eyes, is common for cats. They are in a shallow sleep and are both aware of their surroundings and asleep at the same time in case they need to react to a threat, or a can opener.

Modified Sphinx: Cats will often take a quick nap between activities, doze off watching out the window when nothing is happening outside for example, and assume the modified sphinx position. This is like the lions in front of libraries, sitting with haunches bent, bellies on the ground, and forearms extended in front, tail wrapped along one side. Modified sphinx since domestic cats more often have their front legs slightly tucked in with paws barely showing.

The Sprawl: A cat is at their most vulnerable when lying on their back or side with its belly exposed, so it's a good indicator that they are feeling relaxed and safe and likely in a deep sleep.

A paw across the face is a do not disturb sign, but might also just be trying to block the light. Day sleeping can be hard with the humans bustling about and too much light.

The Twist: Similar to the sprawl but with the upper body curled to one side, hind feet in the air and head cocked or upside down and paws curled forward. Totally irresistible.

Grooming Poses

Watching a cat groom itself and get into the contortions that go along with it can be cute, hilarious, and rather mind-boggling.

- Folded over between the legs to clean privates and tail, and they don't even practice yoga.

- Way too arched neck to clean their ruff, pain in the neck?

- The owl neck twists nearly 180 degrees to reach the back, also a pain in the neck.

- Hands and face the cutest, most child-like so intently repeating.

- The hind leg stretched out like it's ready for shaving. OMG, it's an invitation, right?

- Toes spread, front or back, just have to patty cake with them.

Leonardo da Vinci did dozens of sketches of cats in all sorts of positions and was so enamored of felines that it was rumored he intended to portray the Madonna and child in a painting but holding a cat. The famous quote attributed to him, "Even the smallest feline is a masterpiece of nature" is high praise from the master himself.

Other Purr-fect Poses

The Halloween Arch: Described eloquently by William S. Burroughs, Beat Generation author and artist, a cool cat himself. "A cat's rage is beautiful, burning with pure cat flame, all its hair standing up and crackling blue sparks, eyes blazing and sputtering."

The Drape: Lies across their human's chest

The Nester, also known as Head Warmer: Curls up at the top of the head causing human bed head

The Hanging on for Dear Life: Clinging to their human's chest and over the shoulder (often seen when trying to get your cat into their carrier or taking them out of said carrier at the vet)

The Silhouette: Seen on so many posters they are sitting erect, front legs straight, haunches folded, tail wrapped around—typical of looking out the window or up high surveying their territory.

The Belly

Many cats have a sort of love handles, the jiggly flaps of skin on your cat's belly that can be bait for a hand-mauling, but don't be fooled by the flappy, floppy appearance of the primordial pouch. It is fantastic armor against the most feared cat attack: the bunny kick. Its elasticity protects Kitty's vulnerable underside, by absorbing the energy of powerful kicks and sharp claws. Cat lovers will likely always see those rotund bellies as irresistible to sink their fingers into for a rub or a tickle.

The Pork Chop Thighs

Cats have strange legs. Their knees seem to disappear right into their sides when they sit up, and then stick out when they semi-crouch, making them look like a

Thanksgiving turkey. All we can do is chalk this up to another one of their quirks and snap a few pictures to post online.

Aside from looking adorable, Kitty's big thighs are a powerhouse of energy, the envy of any Russian folk dancer. Have you ever gone down into a crouch and then tried to walk that way? It's hard enough taking just a few steps, but cats do it all day, every day. All felines, including our living room lions, crouch all the time. The size of a big cat's thighs doesn't seem to scale up with their bodies though, making domestic cats all the more special with their succulent pork chop thighs.

Cats were built with speed in mind. They have to be fast, and quiet, to be able to catch prey that can disappear down a hole or escape into the air with a few wingbeats, not to mention those that outrun them, or try to, at least. The average domestic tabby's legs can propel it forward at 30 mph. That's 2 mph faster than the fastest human sprinter. Usain Bolt, eat your heart out.

An ordinary lap cat can jump an astonishing 5–6 times its own height from a sitting start, which is about 6–7 ft high. The human world record holder for high jumping, Javier Sotomayor, did 8 ft 0.46 in, but he had a running start. In 2017, Bud D. Boy, a Siamese cat from Palm Beach did an incredible long jump of 11 ft 2 ½ in, also from a sitting start. It's not as far as the human record of 29 ft 4 1/4 in for a long jump, but that is with a running start.

The Giant Pussy Feet

Have you ever noticed how disproportionate a cat's feet are to the rest of it? We can see how oversized their feet are when they lie feet in the air. In relative terms, the length of a cat's foot is closer to our human shin length than our foot size. Like big clown shoes. An endearing characteristic of this graceful, elegant creature.

We think of a cat's paws as their feet, but there is a little more to it, in fact, a lot more. The paw is more like a cat's toes, with the rest of the foot extending all the way back to the second bend, called the hock. This means that cats slink around on the tips of their toes, a bit like dinosaurs did. No wonder they go about so silently.

Since there is less contact with the ground, they make less noise by walking that way. Furthermore, the pads on cats' paws absorb the impact and sound of a jump incredibly well. They even have sensitive receptors in their toe pads to pick up vibrations, and feel textures and pressure.

Cats mostly sweat from their feet. Sometimes in the summer, you'll notice tiny damp pawprints on glossy surfaces puddy tat has just walked across, waiting to walk across until done being polished.

Cats have five pads, also known as toe beans, on each front paw and four on each hind paw, making 18 toes in total. That fifth toe higher up the arm in the front is called a dewclaw and is almost like a thumb. If it were opposable, our cats would likely get up to far more mischief than they already do. Other animals that also have vestigial dewclaws rarely use them, but cats use them often when playing and climbing, but not as often as the other claws, so they might need more frequent trimming than the other 16 claws.

Front paws are one of the most adorable features of cats and kittens. Where we have long fingers, they have little round toes and they can spread and contract them in the cutest way, especially when startled or playing. This roundness of the fur covered front paws and toes easily makes for the "mittens" association seen in "The Three Little Kittens" classic and many others since. There is no delineation of the parts unless you turn the paw over and Surprise!

Some cats have even more toe beans to love, like the famed Hemingway cats as a result of a congenital physical anomaly called polydactyly. Jake and Paws, the two world record holders for most toes on a polydactyl cat, each have an OMG 28 toes.

Sailors used to believe cats were good luck on an ocean voyage, especially black cats, but polydactyl cats were the jackpot. They were believed to have better balance than other cats because of all the extra toes.

When a cat stands on the full length of its giant feet, it's called a plantigrade stance. When done for a prolonged time it is a symptom of a more serious condition and a vet must examine it to determine the cause, possibly a neurological or musculoskeletal disorder.

The Living End

Fluffy or thin, long or short, cat tails come in many flavors. Aside from its evolutionary advantage of helping a cat balance, helping it stay warm, and improving mobility when hunting, it also serves them in expressing a range of emotions to friends and foes alike. It's like sign language but with tails.

Positive emotions are demonstrated by:

- A fully erect tail is a form of greeting to familiar cats, humans, and other pets.

- A slightly raised and curved tail is a sign that something has piqued the cat's interest.

- A gentle downward curve along the tail with the tip up means the cat is relaxed.

- A tail held to one side is a female in heat inviting a male.

- A swishing tail combined with a lowered posture means the cat is preparing to pounce. The swishing could be to elicit some movement from the target, which helps the cat see it more clearly.

Negative emotions are demonstrated by:

- An unmoving tail with its tip twitching means mild annoyance.

- A whipping tail means the cat is angry.

- A puffed-up tail means the cat is on the defense and is trying to look as big as possible. Usually during a fight.

- A lowered, unmoving tail or a tail tucked between the legs is a sign of complete submission.

A cat's built-in whip is an extension of the spine with give or take 20 flexible tailbones (caudal vertebrae). The exact number of tailbones differs between breeds, with Manx cats having as few as none at all, as it is a genetic defect called Manx syndrome. Bobtail cats have short, kinked tails 1–4 inches long, resembling a bunny's. Even though these cats have short or no tails at all, they are no less mobile than cats with tails because they have had a lifetime to adapt to being without them. A cat that loses its tail can also adapt without it, although it might be a bit clumsy at first.

The domestic cat is the only feline that can hold its tail fully erect while walking. Wild cats can't hold their tails erect like that and will usually have them tucked between their hind legs or let them trail behind them. Well, all the stealth and camouflage in the world won't do you any good if you advertise your presence with a furry flagpole.

Never ever pull a cat's tail. It is very sensitive and has nerves that are directly connected to its bladder and sphincter muscles. A tail injury could lead to temporary or even permanent urinary and fecal incontinence. As Mark Twain said, "A man who carries a cat by the tail learns something he can learn in no other way." What's bad for the cat is worse for the man.

Cat Procreation

Saving the oddest for last believe it or not, cats or as a species, felids, all have the same equipment and mating process. They are the only well-documented species to have all three peculiarities described below, though a small number of other mammals share one or two common characteristics. For those readers who don't want this image in their heads, skip over the rest of this section. Otherwise, here goes.

Induced ovulation, penile spines, copulatory lock. Whew! There are estimated to be around 6,400 mammal species, give or take the constant extinctions and new discoveries, but only cats, from the lion and tiger to the pussy cat, experience all three to make babies. So, the details of what these three aspects of cat intimacy are?

Induced ovulation means there is no cycle for ovulation like there is in women. Eggs are only released by mating. There is estrus in females to attract males when eggs are ready to be released.

Copulatory lock is where things get a bit ugly from the human point of view because male cats have "penile spines" and yes, it is what you think it is. The spines point backward and are made of the same stuff as hair, nails, and skin; keratin. Just like the rough spines on their tongue. Hmm? The penile spines cause the necessary stimulation to induce ovulation which occurs when the penis engorges and the cats are locked together between a minute to an hour—me-owww! Caterwauling? For sure, this is where that word came from. OK. Glad we had the lock and load talk.

As Abraham Lincoln summed it up, "No matter how much cats fight, there always seem to be plenty of kittens."

The Rollercoaster Ride of

Cat Heritage

In ancient times cats were worshipped as gods; they have not forgotten this. –Terry Pratchett

There's a lot of history between the earliest domesticated cats thousands of years ago who earned their keep and the pampered fur babies of today. It might seem like we've had this close relationship with cats forever, but there were bumps along the way.

In the Beginning

In 2004, an archeological discovery of a 9,500-year-old grave was made in Cyprus. An adult human was buried alongside their pet cat, which was treated with the same reverence. This person clearly had a deep emotional bond with their cat, as the two were less than 16 inches apart with both bodies oriented westward. The discovery suggests that the cat, which is not a native species to Cyprus, was intentionally transported from the adjacent Fertile Crescent. Could this be the first "fear of travel" episode in cats?

The discovery pushes our previous estimate for the domestication of cats from 3,600 years ago in Egypt to as far back as the Neolithic Revolution 10,000 years ago and to a humbler island beginning. This coincides with the time when humans first developed agriculture, also known as the First Agricultural Revolution. And where there's agriculture there's pests. Enter the savior cat.

The magic started happening in the Fertile Crescent, a stretch of land in the Middle East spanning from the Mediterranean Sea, crossing North-Eastern Egypt, Jordan, Lebanon, Syria, South-Eastern Turkey, Iraq, and Kuwait to the Persian Gulf. The small, desert-dwelling *Felis silvestris lybica*, commonly known as the African wildcat, discovered that hanging around humans had its benefits, lots of rats, mice, and other pests that plagued the fields and food stores. They might have come for the pests, but benefit two closed the deal, love, and respect from the bi-peds.

Greece

In ancient Greece, cats were associated with the goddess of witches and death, Hecate, because of certain myths. Aristophanes, a Greek playwright who lived in 446–386 BC, was no help and often had cats featured in his works for comedic effect. He coined the phrase "The cat did it" as a means to place the blame. So, that's been going on for nearly 2,000 years when we all know it was the dog. A Greek legend even had a hero cat protecting the infant Jesus from snakes and rats, which greatly increased the cat's standing and earned it a place of honor in the Greek home; but despite this, the honorable cat's alleged connections to witchcraft proved to be too deeply ingrained in the minds of people to forget and adding to that "The cat did it" blame game turned out not funny at all.

Egypt

Millennia-later cats started appearing in art. A statue of a cat carved in ivory from Israel dating back 3,700 years was one of the first clues suggesting that something was afoot (or a-paw). They not only captured our pests, it seemed but also our hearts, their history becoming deeply interwoven with our own. By then they had become a mainstay in our ancestors' daily lives. Not long after, the cat craze swept through Egypt, making the Egyptians the first people to put cat pictures on their walls, 3,600 years before the invention of the Hang In There poster from the '70s and later ad infinitum online postings. It is thanks to the ancient Egyptians that we call the household feline "cat", derived from the North African word for them "quattah". Even the words "Pus" and "Pussy" are derived from "Pasht", another name for Bastet, the fearsome lioness goddess of the sun. Oh, cute little pasht quat!

The Egyptians were the first people to purposefully breed cats and keep them as a form of pest control. Rodents, venomous snakes, and scorpions proved to be no match for the agile felines. So revered were they, that killing a cat became a crime punishable by death (as it should be). A hundred years later, they had attained divinity, with a plethora of gods and mythical beings dedicated to the humans' new feline celebrities. Bastet, Tefnut, Shesemtet, Mafdet, Pakhet, Mut, Sakhmet, and sometimes Wadjet, were Egyptian goddesses, daughters of the Sun God, depicted as cats or having cat heads. It's a common misconception that cats were worshipped in Egypt, but rather, feline attributes were ascribed to these goddesses. The dual nature of cats, that of gentleness and grace combined with aggression and danger is a common theme in ancient Egypt. Even the sun was associated with cats, having both the power to nurture and kill. They were likely also associated with the sun because Egypt had many sunny spots for their divine felines to languish in.

All this love for cats would prove to be somewhat of an Achilles heel to the Egyptians when Cambysess II, the second Achaemenid king of Persia, and less commonly known as "he who will henceforth be called many expletives", attacked the city of Pelusium in 525 BC. He knew just how much the Egyptians venerated cats, and broke his enemies' spirits by chasing cats ahead of his charging horses and literally throwing cats at them. The terrified inhabitants promptly surrendered Pelusium.

It was almost a millennia later when history started taking a grim turn for our beloved felines. In 332 BC, Alexander the Great invaded Egypt and liberated the Egyptians from the Persians. Gone were the days of treating the once-revered cats with the dignity they deserve. Despite the fact that it was still a punishable offense to kill a cat for no reason, a great many catteries were erected to breed cats on a large scale for the purpose of ritual sacrifice and mummification that became the order of the day until Rome conquered Egypt in 30 BC. After that, cats and religion gradually became disassociated, and by 380 AD pagan sacrifices were prohibited and became punishable -sigh- by more death.

Persia

A tale from the *Epic of Kings* of the hero Rostam tells of how the Persian cat came to be. After Rostam saved a magician from robbers he generously offered the man accommodation within his tent. Later, when they were sitting by the campfire under the stars the magician asked Rostam what he desired as a token of his gratitude for saving his life. Rostam claimed that he had everything he could ever want right in front of him: the warmth of the fire, the scent of smoke, and the beauty of the stars above. The wise magician then took a handful of smoke, a dash of flame, and the two brightest stars from the sky and kneaded them all together while he blew on them. When he was done, he held out to Rostam what he didn't know he desired: the very first smoke-gray Persian kitten.

India

Cats were quite revered as hunters and pest controllers and inspired many legends throughout Indian history.

In India we have cats appearing in the two epics of ancient India. In the *Mahabharata,* the mouse Palita helps the cat Lomasa escape from a hunter's trap in exchange for saving the mouse from an owl and a mongoose. They then discuss the nature of relationships in which the power dynamic is skewed. In the other epic, the Ramayana, the god Indra seduces the maid Ahalya, but then transforms into a cat to evade Ahalya's husband. Good choice since he must have needed to sneak away really quietly.

An Indian folktale from the 5th century BC *Panchatantra* even inspired the story of Puss in Boots, although the original was quite different.

China

China had the popular cat goddess Li Shou to whom sacrifices were made for blessings of fertility and pest control. She was the embodiment of the importance of cats in the ancient Chinese creation myth: cats were appointed by the gods to oversee the newly created earth and were given speech, but the cats had better things to do than keeping the world in order and looking after the boring humans, like playing and lying around. The gods repeatedly returned to find the cats idle, doing what cats do best. So, the cats explained to the gods that they were not keen on planetary management. It sounds like a tall order anyway, so the cats suggested that the gods make humans the overseers instead. The gods then took away their speech and gave it to the humans, who did not seem able to understand the gods' commands, while cats remained the masters of time and order. Time to sleep, groom, hunt, and eat in that order.

Europe

The early 13th-century cat became falsely associated with Luciferianism and witchcraft due to the notorious knack people have for shifting the blame. The humor of "the cat did it" was clearly lost on the Europeans and would prove to have terrible consequences for our cat companions. In 1233, Pope Gregory IX issued the Vox in Rama, a papal decree condemning cats for being in league with Satan. He clearly had not heard the Greek legend of the protector cat. The word was passed down through the church to the commoners who believed his papal bull (pun intended) and religious fear mongering ensured the brutalization and slaughter of millions upon millions of cats all across Europe that lasted for centuries. It came back to bite the humans though, as their actions caused rat populations to skyrocket, greatly contributing to and likely even causing the repeated outbreaks of bubonic plague. No one back then saw the correlation between an increase in rats and the spread of the disease, but preferred to continue "blaming the cat".

A common myth that was circulated was that cats stole the breath of life from infants. The fanatics of the day also believed that inhaling just a few strands of a cat's hair would suffocate you (likely the origin of the cat hair causing allergies story we have today), that they had venomous teeth, infectious, consumption-inducing breath, and even poisonous flesh. A 1658 natural historian, Edward Topsel, who was taken much too seriously, wrote that cats were "dangerous to the soul and body" and the familiars of witches. This sealed the fate of old cat ladies throughout Europe of being labeled witches. The early settlers in America brought these fears with them eventually resulting in the infamous Salem witch trials. The ill-treatment of cats and cat ladies continued well into the 19th century until Queen Victoria came along and elevated their standing to levels not seen since ancient Egypt. Long live the Queen, for making cats popular again.

Cat Genetics

In 2000, Carlos A. Driscoll took DNA samples of close to a thousand wildcats and domestic cats from the Middle East, southern Africa, and East Asia. Seven years later, the genetic analysis by Driscoll, Stephen J. O'Brien, and their team was published and revealed that there are five lineages of wildcats:

- *Felis silvestris silvestris*, the European wildcat from Europe.

- *Felis silvestris bieti*, the Chinese mountain cat from China.

- *Felis silvestris ornata*, Asiatic wildcat from Central Asia.

- *Felis silvestris cafra*, Southern African wildcat from southern Africa.

- *Felis silvestris lybica*, African wildcat from northern Africa, the Arabian Peninsula, and the Middle East.

The researcher's findings revealed that not only did the African wildcat's lineage match the subspecies found from Northern Africa to the Caspian Sea, but also all of the domestic cats they tested. That means the common ancestors of our lovable domestic feline furballs all hail from around the Middle East. Why only the African wildcat and none of the other lineages of wildcats were domesticated, is likely due to their proximity to the site of the First Agricultural Revolution. Obviously, cats would have mingled where all the prey of human food were most available.

Recent findings from cat genetics research have shed light on an elusive "new" cat species on the French Mediterranean island of Corsica. It seems to be coming full circle here, as the second mind-blowing discovery from the Mediterranean islands in recent years. The locals have been sharing stories of the enigmatic *ghjattu volpe* or "cat-fox" for hundreds of years that have been reported to attack sheep and goats. This vicious furball seems like a creature straight out of mythology, described as having the fur color and large tail of a fox, but the teeth of a dog.

The first documented sighting was in 1929, but science didn't catch on until nearly a hundred years later when a cat-fox was found while being trapped in a chicken coop. It would seem it's red-handed, too. The 2008 incident spurred the scientific community onto the cat-fox's trail and by 2019, 16 specimens had been found around the island. At first glance, they are hard to distinguish from domestic cats, but their 35-inch long bodies, wide ears, banded tails, dense pest-repellent fur, and enormous, well-developed fangs clearly set these big boys and girls apart. In March 2023, the Biometrics and Evolutionary Biology Laboratory (CNRS—University Claude Bernard Lyon 1) and the French Office for Biodiversity (OFB) confirmed that genetic sampling of the ring-tailed Corsican cat-fox indeed distinguishes it as a unique sub-species of cat.

There is very little change in genetic variation between the different breeds of cats found today and the African wildcat, as no selective breeding had been done up until recently. Why mess with perfection? Because humans are never satisfied. Selective breeding processes have only recently begun producing radically different-looking breeds like Peke-face Persian, Munchkin, Lykoi, Toyger, and LaPerm cats.

Though every new breed of cat seems cuter than the last to some, a few breeders have chosen monetary gain over the welfare of the animals and have resorted to ultra-typing, like over-accentuating a Persian cat's adorable flat face or breeding for even shorter legs on Munchkin cats. Ultra-typing can lead to some serious health issues. Some animal welfare associations however have prohibited breeding for certain traits, and have set standards on what are acceptable traits.

It seems unlikely that cats, who are fiercely territorial and solitary creatures, would have submitted themselves to human subservience. Cats are, after all, the superior species. The other non-cat species we have domesticated had pre-existing dominance hierarchies before their domestication, which means that their obedience is gained by showing them who's boss.

Cats being the proud and willful creatures that they are to this day would never have stood for this. Yet, somehow, cats of the Fertile Crescent began their relationship with humans anyway. There is some evidence that we had struck a mutually beneficial deal with them. Maybe our ancestors saw that they were excellent hunters of mice and other pests and tolerated their caterwauling for that reason. They might be couch potatoes today, but we know that they were and still are natural predators. Another speculation is that they had features so adorable humans couldn't resist them. So, who domesticated who?

Born to Be Wild aka Feral Instincts

To the dismay of many animal lovers and cat owners, cats let outside still hunt prey despite their food bowls being filled to the brim with easy-to-come-by, nutritious food. The occasional dead creature greeting you around the house is an unwelcome sight for some cat owners. Unlike other behaviors that will go away after being spayed or neutered, a cat's hunting instinct is not controlled by hormones and will last its entire life. Trying to train this behavior out of them is not possible though keeping them inside removes most of the stimulus to hunt. So, why do cats still want to hunt?

The typical cat will engage in 3–10 hours of hunting behavior every day, which is a lot, considering they sleep for 12–16 hours a day, not to mention all the time they spend grooming. Masters of time indeed. Simply staring out the window at a bird gets the hunting gears in their little heads turning. They'll express their desire to hunt it with the chattering sound cats universally make when prey is just out of reach. They're basically saying "Lemme at 'em!".

Some of the cute puddy tat behaviors we love stem from their hunter's instincts. For instance, when cats play, they bat toys back and forth and throw them in the air. This is not for our amusement though. One theory is that domestic cats let out all their repressed hunting instincts that way. Another theory is that cats do this to daze and avoid being bitten by their prey. Both seem likely, whereas cats in the wild have more manners and don't play with their food, except when training their kittens, house cats have become rather sadistic torturers when they occasionally catch prey— it's just another toy. Is your puddy tat catch-and-release kitty or psycho-killer kitty?

Cats often pull hard when chomping down on their toys and pull or lick at the stuffing. This is similar to their behavior when pulling at the skin, fur, or feathers while tearing into a fresh kill. By the way, toss the toy out once it's been eviscerated, the stuffing is likely not safe for your little predator to be playing with.

One can even see their wild nature when they refuse to eat their food. It's not a rebellious streak coming through but is likely a behavioral adaptation to vary their diet and not get too used to hunting the same prey all the time. At least one species is trying not to deplete its resources.

Felines have honed their hunting skills over millions of years. Domestic cats have inherited all of their ancestors' instincts to stalk, hunt, and kill. Even though their lives of comfort no longer require them to hunt, they still enjoy the thrill of it. It's a natural, rewarding experience for them, and is a lot like the feeling we humans get when participating in competitive sports. That killer instinct has been softened which is a major reason they have become such popular pets. Humans have a fascination with predators, perhaps because they too were once prey. So, having a little predator living in the house is a continual thrill because they have chosen us, chosen not to attack but to love us and allow us to love them. Though some of a cat's outward appearance has changed, our sleek and agile pets are very much the same as they were close to a million years ago. Their bodies are built for hunting: long teeth for a lethal bite, strong jaws to hold their prey, sharp claws to grab a hold of prey and climb up trees, soft padding under their paws for stealthy stalking, and more.

Today, we substitute elements of their natural environment with cat towers, scratching posts, and toys to serve as an outlet for their natural instincts, to keep them content, and to preserve our skin.

Cats are tertiary consumers on the food chain, being both the hunters and the hunted. They are obligate carnivores, or hypercarnivores, which means their diets consist of at least 70% meat. No carbs for these guys. In the wild, cats hunt small mammals, insects, birds, reptiles, and the occasional fish, though the latter will require them to get over their dislike of water. A cat's prey will often have food in its stomach, and cats don't seem to mind the extra stuffing.

Feral cats threaten many wild reptile and bird populations, which are now in decline. Small mammals, like rats, mice, and other rodents are preferable to the ferals, but they'll try to catch pretty much anything they want. It's literally a living. Keeping cats indoors will make little difference to the decline of other species though, as feral cat populations vastly outnumber pet cat populations, but it will greatly increase your cat's lifespan and keep it from getting into trouble.

How Cats Cast Their Spell

on Us

A cat is actually a perfect pet. You get the love and companionship of a creature covered in fur, and you don't have to take it for a walk, and it can feed itself. Less maintenance. Surely any man can appreciate the practicality of this choice. —
Iliza Shlesinger

Cat-titude

There is much mystery surrounding cats, and millennia of co-existing with them have not solved that mystery. In our inability to know them, we anthropomorphize them, give them human characteristics to put an understandable-to-us label on them; an unknowable attitude that humans perceive as a whole host of different things depending on the person relating to them.

Superior, selective, mysterious, intelligent, psychic, manipulative, haughty, aloof, and loving have all been used to describe our pussy cats, a rather incongruous collection of perceptions. We project these qualities on cats as if they were humans and have always done so as a variety of intelligent folks have said.

Appearance

Soft, silky fur over a lithe, graceful body, topped with triangular ears and nose on a triangular head, in which sit two extraordinarily beautiful, big, iridescent eyes; and it is all atop plump, little, round pink pads on quiet feet with outrageous tufts of hair sprouting between the toes. Nothing is more soothing and gratifying than when this velvety being leaps onto your lap, curls itself into a warm ball, and begins to gently rumble. Then the arm connected to those fabulous soft pads stretches up to gently touch your face and those jewel-tone eyes close slowly in bliss. Heart-melting; how could you not fall in love?

Every person has their own opinion on why they love their cat(s). Whether it's their soft fluffiness, their clownish behavior, their adorable little faces, or something else entirely, there are some reasons that are unanimous among cat parents.

Their sleek, supple bodies are definitely one of the best things about cats. Watching them traverse the domestic landscape is mesmerizing. The way they climb, jump, and play with effortless grace is truly a thing to behold. It's like having a wildlife show with fearsome, little-big cats performing right in your living room. Somehow, the clumsy adorable antics of kittens change into the elegant and mysterious cat.

Sleek cats and chubby cats alike just beg to be petted (but only when they want to be petted). Their silky fur, which makes them look bigger, only makes it more irresistible to reach out and pet, sinking fingers into all that fluffiness. When they curl up nose to tail to sleep, making the classic donut shape, it not only provokes a coo of delight from us, it keeps them nice and warm and their organs well protected. It would be nearly criminal to disturb their peaceful slumber but we do it anyway and they forgive us.

Studies have revealed that people who were shown pictures of very cute kittens and puppies prior to playing the game Operation were more careful than test groups who were shown pictures of moderately cute kittens and puppies. Their findings proved that people are biased toward the cuter versions, have an increased willingness to care for and protect them, and have a decreased likelihood of aggression toward them. This is termed the baby schema response and is important for an infant's survival. Cats and kittens have some features similar to those of human babies, and it brings out a strong desire to take care of them, despite their decidedly independent nature. Human children as young as 3–6 years already show a preference for baby-like features. Our innate caretaking desires are part of what fuels our love for them, as it serves to forge the bond between cat parent and cat, as it does between human children and their parents.

The fact that the use of the term "fur baby" has become so widespread is a simple testament to that bond. The little faces in disproportionately large heads, large eyes, small button noses, small mouths (unless they yawn), and the fetal curl when they sleep, are just the tip of what makes them decidedly baby-like.

We didn't really need scientists to point this obvious one out to us, but research has shown that cat meows can be similar to a human baby's cries. What is interesting though is that domestic cats have a more infantile, less scary, and generally more pleasant sound than their wild counterparts. What's even more interesting is that by observing us, cats have learned to attune specific frequencies so they can imitate the sounds our babies make in order to get our attention. So clever. Kittens meow to their mothers to communicate their needs though adult cats rarely meow at other cats and reserve their meows for humans which suggests that they see us as parents.

The way we use baby talk with our cats, called pet-directed-speech, to get their attention is just like our habit of doing so with our human babies and evokes a response from our fur babies as well. All this suggests that we might have picked them as our companions for these baby-like features.

Comfort

Then there is the purr. There are few things quite as soothing as the purring of a contented cat. Not only is it pleasant to hear, but it has plenty of benefits for the ones blessed by the good vibrations. There's nothing quite like being comforted by your feline companion purring next to or in your lap in times of sickness and sadness.

When the going gets rough, or even when lounging in your favorite chair, your trusty pussy cat can be counted on to warm your lap, especially in those chilly winter months. It's a comfort to both cat and keeper alike to share a space and a touch, even if one or both are in blissful slumber.

Loneliness has existed as long as life has but is an epidemic in modern times with all the freedoms and advancements that have created more leisure but not provided more or improved relationships. There is less and less human contact, zoom calls, texting, video gaming, etc. replacing meaningful relationships. Even in 1928, when the first American picture book for children was published, *Millions of Cats* by Wanda Gág, it expressed the need for a cat to assuage loneliness. The book begins:

> *"Once upon a time there was a very old man and a very old woman. They lived in a nice clean house that had flowers all around it except, where the door was. But they couldn't be happy because they were so very* **lonely**. *"If only we had a cat!" sighed the very old woman."*

Well, the very old man eventually brings one home and they live happily ever after. In the lonely moments that every human being experiences, cat lovers have the comfort of our baby beasties purring in our arms. We are definitely not lonely.

Low Maintenance

Another reason cats are so easy to love is they tend to be low maintenance. They like to play intensely the hunter/prey game whether with a little catnip mouse or a hairy-looking toy dangling in the doorway. We often hear these goings on in the other room at night so cats entertain themselves without having to have their human interact. That's not to say humans joining in with a feather or wand toy aren't great fun but they are capable of entertaining themselves.

Cats sleep a lot. They don't need baths like the barking pet varieties do, they pretty much take care of that themselves unless climbing through the cupboard they knock the syrup over and don't get away fast enough. Quite rare.

Cat independence is a low-maintenance trait of our feline friends we appreciate. They don't require walks around the block, and all the exercise they need to stay fit and healthy can be given to them from the couch with the flick of a cat wand. They don't need much from us, heck, they don't really need us at all. The enormous populations of feral cats worldwide are a testament to that. However, our own pampered pussycats do require a bit more from us. When they're not hounding us to top up their food bowls, they usually go off on their own to do mysterious cat things.

If not for a litter box or window access they might have been yowling to be let out all the time, but they manage with what's available.

Though cats are independent, they do see us as a source of great security and comfort, not just as the food provider. A 2019 study concluded that our fur babies see us as parents. This checks off the "need to nurture" box for cat parents. The researchers observed how cats behaved in three stages: in an unfamiliar room with their owners, then alone in the room, and then again when their owners returned. Upon the owner's return, the cats displayed a similar secure attachment level that human children do, by going back and forth between the owners and exploring the unfamiliar room.

Mystery

I wish that my writing was as mysterious as a cat. –Edgar Allan Poe

How many times have people assumed incorrectly about another person that they acted so superior, for instance, and after getting to know them better they find out it was shyness or putting a façade over their inferiority complex? Not to imply that cats might have inferiority complexes (although who knows?), but rather consider that they are not knowable. It may be that cats perceive us as mysteries as well, by the way they can tilt their head as if questioning, then stare us down in a way that feels like they are trying to figure us out. Another projection? A possibility?

Perhaps a wonderful thing cats offer us is the opportunity to flex our intuitive (some would say psychic) senses. After all, one of the traits of cat lovers is sensitivity. If so, maybe all the different perceptions are correct and cats are as complex as we are.

Mystery is not a bad thing evidenced by the number of mystery novels that are read. Mysteries and romance novels are the two bestselling books and a romance with mystery equals life with a cat.

Intelligence

I have studied many philosophers and many cats. The wisdom of cats is infinitely superior. –Hippolyte Taine

Given the highly intelligent list of cat owners, it's not surprising that cat parents appreciate how smart their fur kids are. Non-cat parents can easily be fooled into thinking cats aren't smart when they don't obey but we know what's going on. They're considering and choosing, their choices reflecting their independence. Cats are considered to have the mental acuity of a two-year-old human child. We often think of cats as another trainable animal and yes, they certainly can be, but they choose it. If they don't want to do something, they won't, and you'll never know for sure why not. Cats can be obstinate as well as compliant and like their human parents, each is unique, which makes for a more interesting relationship.

In 2017, researchers in South Australia and New Zealand consolidated the data from an earlier survey with 2,291 cat lovers about their 2,802 pet cats. They identified five distinct personality types in cats based on the Five-Factor Model used for humans, and called it the *Feline Five*:

- Agreeableness: How affectionate and friendly a cat is to people, and how gentle its nature is.

- Dominance: How much of a bully a cat is, how aggressive it is towards people and other cats, and whether it's trying to assert dominance over other cats.

- Extraversion: How adventurous, alert, inquisitive, and smart a cat is.

- Impulsiveness: How erratic a cat's behavior is and how unobservant it is in its surroundings.

- Neuroticism: How shy, insecure, and anxious, the cat behaves and how suspicious and fearful it is of people.

These personality types and traits are by no means all. They mimic the various human personality typing such as the Myers-Briggs groupings. There can be many shades of each and combinations of types. The Agreeable Neurotic is the classic combo of a once feral cat adopted by a human rescuer(s). They may be very agreeable with their human saviors but when a stranger enters the house they disappear under the bed.

So, how smart are cats? A cat's brain makes up 0.9% of its body weight, and a dog's is 1.2% of its body weight, whereas ours is 2%, but relative brain size isn't the best indicator of intelligence. Take sperm whales for instance, we know they are highly intelligent from their sophisticated social behaviors and vocal communication, but their brains are only 0.02% of their body weight. It's the neurons or nerve cells in the brain that count.

The surface folding and structure of a cat's cerebral cortex are 90% similar to our own. This is the region of the brain that stores short- and long-term memory and governs higher functions of rational thought and problem-solving. Even though a cat's brain is smaller than a dog's, a cat's cerebral cortex has 300 million neurons, nearly twice the amount a pooch has (160 million neurons). Can that mean cats are almost twice as smart as dogs?

Research has shown that it takes cats only one experience to be able to remember and apply information from that memory. They learn by watching and doing, just like us, and they're great at it. They just don't cooperate very well when it comes to testing them. One behavioral experiment testing the short-term memory of dogs and cats showed that cats remembered where food was hidden for 16 hours after being shown once, whereas the dogs couldn't remember after 5 minutes. Furthermore, cats can remember what happened and where it happened for 10 years or longer but it doesn't mean they can't forget. Poet Pam Brown remarked on cat intelligence this way, "Cats can work out mathematically the exact place to sit that will cause the most inconvenience."

Clean

Cleanliness ranks high in the desirability of a cat. Cats spend such an inordinate amount of time grooming themselves, that one would think they're preparing for a royal engagement. It might seem like an awful lot of grooming, but it is essential. Cats are very clean creatures and they do have a lot of fur to get around to. Despite the fact that they are covering their fur in saliva, their spiky tongues give their skin a good deep scrubbing.

Over-grooming can cause bare patches, even "hot" spots, and be an indicator of anxiety, allergies, or other conditions that a vet should be consulted about. If you think your cat is overgrooming and consuming an excessive amount of hair, use a hairball treatment regularly to prevent an emergency from accumulated hair in the stomach that can't be passed or vomited.

Burying their scat is also a bonus, though it's technically just "swept under the rug", it's the thought that counts. The likelihood of stepping on a cat landmine is drastically reduced since they keep all their business localized to the litter box or some sandy corner in the yard. However, if your cat is mad at you, you just might find that landmine on your bed or favorite chair.

Quiet

*The ideal of calm exists in a sitting ca*t. –Jules Renard

Then there's the quiet quality of the pussy cat. Have you ever stepped backward and accidentally trod on your cat's toe or tail because you didn't hear it? Being stealthy has helped cats survive for thousands of years, considering where they are on the food chain, they must have been sneaking about 24/7. Not being eaten and not alerting your prey while sneaking up on it ranks high on a cat's list of priorities, so it stands to reason that they would try not to draw attention to themselves, thus their equipment includes soft, silent feet. A quiet roommate is a good roommate. The creator of the Linux software kernel, Linus Torvalds said, "I want my office to be quiet. The loudest thing in the room —by far—should be the occasional purring of the cat."

Chosen

It is no compliment to be the stupidly idolized master of a dog whose instinct it is to idolize, but it is a very distinct tribute to be chosen as the friend and confidant of a philosophic cat who is wholly his own master and could easily choose another companion if he found such an one more agreeable and interesting. –H.P. Lovecraft

Importantly, cats make their humans feel chosen. Most people would say that playing favorites is rude, but cats don't have that concept. There is a certain smug satisfaction when a cat walks by several other laps to come sit in yours. You have been granted a great honor and can claim in-cat-pacitation when asked to do anything. Being chosen by your cat is a privilege we enjoy earning. There are many quotes from unknowns, probably everyday cat lovers expressing the same thing, the specialness of being the chosen one.

Cats of the Rich and Famous

As every cat owner knows, nobody owns a cat. –Ellen Perry Berkeley

The personalities and professions of cat owners are quite varied but all have a soft spot for the pussy cat. Some of the rich and famous went to great lengths for them, some might say overboard. It's not surprising so many of those included are writers since they tend to put much of their life down in words, including cat stories, and what better to write about or to serve as a muse than a cat? However, while famed cat lovers are heavily represented in the arts from writers to painters, singers, and actors, there are also the compassionate and powerful. To further expound on those who love cats, think about the traits of these well-known cat lovers. Do you identify with some of them?

The Compassionate

Nurse Florence Nightingale had a passion for caring not only for the ill but also for the 60 or so cats she owned throughout her life. She spoiled all her cats rotten, having them dine on specially made food served on China plates, but her favorite cat, Mr. Bismarck, ate on schedule every evening and would even enjoy a little rice pudding with dinner. Miss Nightingale often wrote about her cats in letters and correspondences, and some of her notes have telltale smudges and pawprints inked onto the pages and immortalized for future generations to adore. She said, "Cats possess more sympathy and feeling than human beings."

The Prophet Mohammed loved every cat he came across, but adored his cat Muezza and would drink water from the same vessel she had drunk from, despite what others thought about it. One day he was called to prayer and found Muezza sleeping on the sleeve of his robe. He wanted to wear the robe to offer prayer, but rather than disturbing her slumber, he cut the sleeve off the robe!

Animal Rights Activist and actor Ian Somerhalder, Founder of the Ian Somerhalder Foundation which fights against animal cruelty and addresses environmental issues, loves all his animals and his three cats named Mokuleiya, Thursday Adams, and Sohalier.

The Powerful

A cat doesn't care if you are smart or dumb, give him your heart and he will give you his. —Abraham Lincoln

President Abraham Lincoln was once given two cats as a present. Tabby and Dixie, as he named them, were probably the first cats to grace the halls of the White House with their presence. Lincoln was fond of opening the doors of the White House to homeless cats after so thoroughly being smitten by the first and second cats of the United States. He became nothing short of obsessed with his cats and doted on them without caring about what anyone else thought, even feeding Tabby from the table with a golden fork during a state dinner. When he was admonished by his wife for doing so, he replied: "If the gold fork was good enough for President James Buchanan, I think it is good enough for Tabby." He became so frustrated by his own Cabinet, that once he was heard saying: "Dixie is smarter than my whole cabinet! And furthermore, she doesn't talk back!"

Among his numerous quotes about cats, one, in particular, must have brought a tear to many a military man. While visiting General Ulysses S. Grant at an army headquarters during the last days of the Civil War, he found three stray kittens. He promptly put them in his lap and while tenderly cleaning their eyes with his handkerchief, said: "Kitties, thank God you are cats, and can't understand this terrible strife that is going on." Maybe it's not too late to petition for three grateful

Georgia marble kittens to be added to Lincoln's lap at the Lincoln Memorial.

After Lincoln, some of the succeeding U.S. presidents and their families kept to the tradition of keeping cats in the White House namely, Theodore Roosevelt, Woodrow Wilson, Calvin Coolidge, John F. Kennedy, Gerald Ford, Jimmy Carter, Bill Clinton, George W. Bush and Joe Biden.

Queen Victoria of Great Britain owned many animals but loved her Blue Point Persians the most. White Heather, a fluffy white cat, was her favorite. At the Queen's behest, Her Majesty White Heather was to continue a life of opulence and comfort in Buckingham Palace. After Queen Victoria passed away, White Heather did just that for the remainder of her days. Talk about spoiled.

Catherine the Great of Russia had two colonies of cats at the Winter Palace, situated in St. Petersburg, during the 18th century. Of all her cats her favorite breed was the Russian Blue, which she often gifted to other monarchs as pets. These precious pusses lived with her on the upper floors of the palace. Catherine even promoted the working cats she employed in the basement, dubbing them official guards, and giving them extra rations and even salaries.

The Writers

Writer Ernest Hemingway had a white oddball named Snow White who had six toes on each of her front paws. She was the first of many generations of polydactyl cats the proud cat daddy Hemingway owned.

Hemingway's cats, as they are called today, are all descended from Snow White and all carry the same polydactyl gene. The clowder of six-toed cats that still roam the grounds of the Ernest Hemingway Home and Museum make up half of the fifty or more cats. All Hemingway's cats are well cared for and when they pass, they are buried in the garden behind the house.

Writer Mark Twain loved cats more than he loved people, as is the case with many cat lovers around the world. He owned nineteen cats at one time and would rent cats whenever he was away from home. Rent-a-Cat? When his cat Bambino went missing, he placed ads in various newspapers offering a $5 reward to anyone who found him, that's roughly $130 today. Bambino returned on his own a few days later, but opportunists kept turning up, even after Twain had again placed ads notifying the public of his return. If he were alive today, Mr. Twain would most certainly have written his bestsellers from the comfort of a cat café.

Writer Jirō Osaragi looked after and fed hundreds of homeless cats that would show up at his residence in Kamakura, Japan. The Osaragi Jirō Memorial Museum in Yokohama, Japan, is dedicated to the life and works of this great Shōwa-period author and feline ally. The museum not only features his manuscripts and paraphernalia from his life but is also adorned with a great many cat sculptures and artworks. It's a must-see for all cat lovers passing through Yokohama.

Writer Louisa May Alcott, the author of Little Women, was a self-professed cat lady who included cats in her works. She even penned a heartfelt poem about the death of her beloved cat S. B. Pat Paw.

Writers Anne, Emily, and Charlotte Brontë had a great fondness for their cats, Black Tom and Tiger, the former of which was their favorite. According to Ellen Nussey, a close friend of the girls, Black Tom was spoiled and treated so well that he gradually entered a state of opulent friendliness and satisfaction.

Writer Haruki Murakami, bestselling author, and Jazz enthusiast, named his Tokyo jazz club after his cat, Peter Cat. Murakami's books always feature a cat slinking into and out of his characters' lives. He said "I collect records. And cats. I don't have any cats right now. But if I'm taking a walk and I see a cat, I'm happy."

"Kittens believe that all nature is occupied with their diversion" was observed by French writer F. A. Paradis de Moncrif, best known for his work *Les Chats* published in 1727. It is an early investigation of the part cats played in society. As is often the case with new ideas, he was frequently ridiculed by fellow writers for his deep interest in cats. Since then, *Les Chats* has become a renowned resource on cats.

Beat Generation author William S. Burroughs said, "The cat does not offer services. The cat offers itself. Of course, he wants care and shelter. You don't buy love for nothing."

Sixteenth-century writer Michel de Montaigne who popularized the essay genre wrote, "When I play with my cat, who knows whether she is not amusing herself with me more than I with her."

The Painters

Artist Pablo Picasso, the famous cubist artist had a cat named Minou, his "mews", you could say. His 1939 painting *Cat Catching a Bird* features a scruffy cat rendered in a sand-paint mix. It looks particularly vicious with its oversized nails, eyes, and the bird's damaged wing accented with white. The subject was somewhat of an obsession to him, and it is thought to represent the conflicts around the build-up of the Second World War. Other masters of visual art who were cat lovers include Salvador Dali, Gustav Klimt, Henri Matisse, Andy Warhol, Wassily Kandinsky, Georgia O'Keeffe, and Pierre Bonnard.

Artist Louis Wain was a Victorian-era visual artist who deserves an extra-special mention for his numerous works depicting humorous anthropomorphized cats parodying everyday human activities, like playing golf or cricket, riding bicycles, or flying a kite. Louis and his wife Emily Richardson found a stray black-and-white kitten one rainy night and called him Peter. Peter served as the inspiration behind most of Louis's illustrations and paintings. Peter comforted Emily when she fell ill with breast cancer, and Louis would sketch hilarious works of Peter for his wife's amusement. Emily encouraged him to publish his work, but shortly after his first works were published, she passed away. Louis fell into a deep depression and poverty despite his popularity. He was committed to an asylum as his mental state seemed to deteriorate.

Louis became obsessed with drawing cats and many of his works featured his beloved muse, Peter. He started experimenting with cubism and a more abstract, psychedelic art style. His doctors ascribed his drastic change in style to his alleged schizophrenia, yet there was no deterioration of his skill and he continued producing work after work of splendidly drawn cats. Louis would later attribute the foundation and early success of his career all to Peter. Today, Louis is considered an eccentric genius who changed the public's opinion of cats through humor. Our hats go off to Peter for being the absolute best boy and inspiring a career.

Both artist and humorist, Jim Davis, cartoonist, and creator of Garfield wrote, "Way down deep, we're all motivated by the same urges. Cats have the courage to live by them."

The Singers and Songwriters

Singer and songwriter Freddie Mercury, the legendary frontman of Queen, had a deep love for his cats and is believed to have given a room to each of them in his London mansion. His love of cats started when his girlfriend, Mary Austen bought them two cats named Tom and Jerry. They surely must have realized the irony of calling a cat Jerry. When he was away on tour, Freddie would call home to talk to each of his cats in turn. He owned a total of ten cats and would spoil them rotten, with freshly prepared fish or chicken more often than not, and even giving each of his cats a Christmas stocking of their own. The song, Delilah, was written as a tribute to his most beloved cat.

Some other notable musicians include:

- Singer and songwriter Taylor Swift calls her three adorable cats Benjamin Button, Meredith Grey, and Olivia Benson.

- Singer Katy Perry owned a pretty kitty named Kitty Perry, who sadly passed after 15 years of companionship with her superstar mom.

- Singer and songwriter Ed Sheeran is a vocal feline lover who cares deeply for his two cats, Dorito and Calippo.

- Singer Britney Spears adores her Bengal named Wendy.

The Actors

Doris Day, an American actress who exploded onto the silver screen in the mid-40s, and continued to rake in the roles for decades after, was an avid advocate in the animal welfare community and a cat lover. Doris established the Doris Day Pet Foundation in 1978, which strove to help animals and the people who care for them. It later became the Doris Day Animal Foundation (DDAF) as its efforts to protect animals became more far-reaching. Up until her death in 2019, Doris was closely involved with the DDAF.

- Actor Salma Hayek rescued an ark of more than thirty animals including many cats. She hoards and loves them on her ranch in Washington State.

- Actor Nicole Kidman rescued a black and white kitty named Louis to join her other two cats named Ginger and Snow.

- Actor Robert Downey Jr. is a cat daddy with two beautiful cats named Montgomery and Dartanian

- Actor Kate Beckinsale loves her rambunctious cat Willow and often dresses up her 12-year-old Persian named Clive.

- Actor Mark Ruffalo is smitten with his five cats named Inky, Hansel, Biscotti, Felix, and Magnus.

- Drew Barrymore, actor, and homeless animal advocate rescued her three fur children named Fern, Lucky, and Peach.

- Actor and singer Jennifer Lopez added an adorable Devon Rex named Hendrix to her family.

- Actor Cameron Diaz dresses her white cat named Little Man in fashionable attire for outings.

- Actor and model Gilles Marini lets his daughter's precious Persian cat, Penelope, roam the house freely with his many other adopted pets.

- Celebrity personality, cook, designer, author, and businessperson, Martha Stewart, has owned more than 20 cats in the past four decades.

Sports Icons:

Mario Andretti, champion driver of Indy 500, Daytona 500, Le Mans, and too many others to name is quoted as saying "Everything comes to those who wait...except a cat." Seems waiting is an odd thing to occupy the mind of a racer but not a cat lover.

There are a great many more important figures who loved and kept cats in recorded history and millions more regular people who had important cats. The lives of those unsung feline heroes who rid the farms and castles, barns and seafaring ships, stables, and palaces are all inextricably tied to our history. Cats are as much part of the great civilization we have today as those down through history, pampered and petted. With the advent of the internet, we are seeing just how many millions of people love cats today, and throughout history, it's obvious that there have always been cat lovers.

The IT Factor

Although dogs seem to get the limelight more often than the house cat, there are plenty of beloved cat characters of fame in comics, books, and movies, and don't forget the civilizations that worshiped them. Most dog roles in movies are as rescuers or are figuring out how to get home (Snoopy is an exception).

As you can see from the list below, cats are far more diverse and have more range.

- Filch's cat, Mrs. Norris from the *Harry Potter* series

- Hermine's cat, Crookshanks also from *Harry Potter*

- *Puss-in-Boots* from literature and movies

- Holly GoLightly's Cat (also known as Orangey) from Breakfast at Tiffany's

- Mr. Jinx the toilet-using cat from *Meet the Parents*

- The Cheshire Cat from Lewis Carroll's *Alice in Wonderland*

- Garfield from the cartoon strip created by Jim Davis

- Felix the Cat from Pat Sullivan and Otto Messmer animated cartoons, first feline silent film star, 1919

- Hobbes from Calvin and Hobbes cartoon strip by Bill Watterson

- Snowbell from the children's book *Stuart Little*

- *The Cat in the Hat* from Dr. Seuss' children's book

- Bastet, a cat goddess worshipped by ancient Egyptians

- Mr. Mistoffelees from T.S. Elliot's *Old Possum's Book of Practical Cats* (and Broadway show *Cats*)

- Graymalkin from Shakespeare's *MacBeth*

- Buttercup from *The Hunger Games*

- Bob from the movie *A Street Cat Named Bob*

- Milo from the movie *The Adventures of Milo and Otis*

- Ulysses from the movie *Inside Llewyn Davis*

- Tonto from the movie *Harry & Tonto*

- Thomasina from the Disney movie *The Three Lives of Thomasina*

- Tao from the book and movie *The Incredible Journey*

- Figaro from *Pinocchio*

- Pyewacket from the *Bell, Book and Candle*

So, another reason we love cats? They have become an integral part of the fabric of modern society as well as our individual lives and they have that "IT" movie star quality.

Charm Your Way into Your

Cat's Heart

We call ourselves a dog's 'master'—but whoever dared to call himself the 'master' of a cat? We own a dog—he is with us as a slave and inferior because we wish him to be. But we entertain a cat—he adorns our hearth as a guest, fellow-lodger, and equal because he wishes to be there. –H.P .Lovecraft

Cats love those that love them in the way they want to be loved. Yes, there are things you can do for and with your cat to create a fulfilling life for them especially if they are primarily indoors. More about that later. But cats can, at a minimum, tell if someone is a good or bad person and will never trust or bond closely with someone they deem bad if they will even stay with them for long. So, being a good person is a good start to earning a cat's trust and affection. Newscaster Jane Pauley said, "Never trust a man who hates cats." Your cat probably won't like them either.

Personal values aren't talked about much anymore. Hear the word value and think, a good deal for the money, is how it's primarily used today and that is not the right meaning in this case. It's an ethical code lived by a person with values such as treating people only the way you'd like to be treated; with kindness, patience, courtesy, respect, honesty, interest, consideration, etc.

It's hard to know for sure if one of these is valued more than anything else by cats, but respect has to be near the top. Showing respect with regard to a cat is letting it set boundaries and then honoring those boundaries. Sounds rather human and the way it should be. Boundaries include not interrupting their grooming, sleeping, and especially eating. Not forcing them to do anything that is not for their own good/safety like making them stay on your lap when they don't want to or carrying them over to meet a new person; they should decide on their own if they want to be near a person. Some cats just don't like being carried. Respect that.

Yes, there are times when carrying is necessary for their own good such as going to the vet or administering medication. If they like being picked up, make sure to support them with both arms, no dangling the cat.

Another form of respect cats appreciate is cited by a famous Sci-Fi author Robert A. Heinlein "Anyone who considers protocol unimportant has never dealt with a cat." Cats like regular schedules for things like meals especially. They will adapt to irregularities but respecting their mealtime protocols will earn points with your cat. Meals for cats should be in a relatively quiet, low-traffic area.

Cats are fastidious, obviously apparent in their constant grooming, but also in their toilet habits. As comedian Rodney Dangerfield joked: "When I played in the sandbox, the cat kept covering me up." So, as previously noted, keeping that litter box clean will also be appreciated by your puddy tat.

Adoration goes a long way to securing the affection and love of a cat, after all, they were once worshipped. Cats do like worshipping and it's luckily a natural tendency of cat lovers as noted by famed horror/weird fiction author, H. P. Lovecraft, "The cat is such a perfect symbol of beauty and superiority that it seems scarcely possible for any true aesthete and civilized cynic to do other than worship it."

Know Your Cat's Purr-sonal Preferences for Giving Affection Without Getting Clawed

To Hold or Not to Hold

Holding a cat should be left up to the cat. Some perceive it as a threat, and restraint, and will struggle to get away, especially a former feral or poorly socialized cat. The rule with cats, let them decide. Even those who like being held, only do so when they want, not at your pleasure. They typically like to be held against the chest or over the shoulder like a baby being burped. When holding your pussy cat, always use one hand or arm to support their feet or bottom, the other arm around the body, with your hand resting on the upper back or cupping the neck. Never try to hold them belly up, like a cradled baby; too vulnerable. Hold firmly but not tightly. Like the thunder shirt wrapped around a pet to reduce anxiety, it's not too tight or too loose, just like your arms should be.

Forcing a cat is a sure way to alienate its affection and even make it run away from the "abuser" in the cat's eyes. If a cat allows holding, at the first sign of restlessness or movement to leave, let go immediately. Over time, the cat will learn it's not going to be restrained and can trust to be freed as soon as it wants. When trust is established, the cat may allow holding for longer intervals and seek it out more often. Gaining the trust of a cat and having it seek out your arms is truly an honor.

Brushing

Brushing a cat will produce a static charge, and likely a purr, but be careful if you want to go in for a bop on the nose, as it might give your cat a shock and startle them. Many cats require frequent brushing to prevent their fur from becoming tangled, or worse, matted. Most cats love being brushed though, and will get quite used to being pampered. Brush gently and stop if the pussy cat signals to stop.

Brushing your cat serves to help them shed the undercoat faster, which provides some relief in the hotter months of the year. Your cat will also have fewer hairballs as a result.

Petting

There's kind of a toll you have to pay with a cat; if you don't pet her for 10 minutes, she'll bother you for six hours. —Scott Adams

As with brushing, stroking fur produces a static charge. Stroke slowly, gently, and with the grain. Most cats won't appreciate having their fur stroked against the grain and will become agitated and might lash out. An alternative to stroking is burying your fingers in their fur and softly flexing your fingers open and closed which generates far less static.

Pay attention to signs that the cat likes or dislikes what you are doing. Good signs include purring, nudging your hand, rubbing up against you, and kneading. It might be doing one or a few of these at once. If a cat's not enjoying the petting, it might pull back or flatten its ears. You might notice it cringing, which usually means you're touching its whiskers or another sensitive area.

Also keep an eye on their tail, as they will express how they feel about being petted in a particular way. If their tail slowly and gently curls at the tip, they are enjoying it, but if the entire tail starts swinging, jerking, or repeatedly whips against a surface, then they are not a fan of your technique and have had enough. Best to stop at this point, as the cat is already annoyed and no amount of petting is going to fix it, but please try again later.

Each new cat is a journey of discovery. If it's not giving you overtly bad signals like flattening its ears, but you're unsure whether it's okay to pet it, ask it for permission. It will likely be watching your eyes to gauge your intent. Soften your eyes and offer it a slow blink. Don't stare too long at them as they'll see it as a threat. Don't move too fast, but casually extend a hand at an oblique angle towards a spot near it. Reaching straight for it is also threatening. Now, wait for it to come to you. You can offer it words of encouragement, but be nonchalant. It will either back off, or it will approach and sniff your hand. If it rubs a cheek on your hand, you've experienced a special moment. Don't be too eager though, and allow it to lead the interaction. Congratulations, you've made a new furry friend.

Every cat has their own favorite spots where they love to be petted. Even your fluffy lap warmer of several years might occasionally surprise you by suddenly being into a spot that used to be taboo, like its paws or belly.

Scratches are also much appreciated by our feline companions, with some of the more common spots being under the chin, behind the ears, the forehead between the eyes, and the cheeks behind their whiskers. Occasionally they like to be petted on the lower back. Pause every few seconds to see if the cat is still enjoying it. If they want more they will rub up against you or your hand, nudging you to go on. They especially love it if they are leaning into your touch, and might lose their balance momentarily if you pull your hand away. They won't mind if you resume, and let's face it, you want to.

Cats also love the occasional massage. Like us, they also carry some tension in their muscles. Every cat has its own sweet spots but it's best not to overdo it. A gentle paw massage while they quietly lie is sometimes acceptable, but take care not to go too fast. Ease them into the feeling by softly squeezing the pads. If they like it, they'll part their toe-beans so you can get in between them. Try softly rolling the loose skin by its shoulder blades and the scruff of its neck between your fingers, pressing down lightly on the muscle. Some cats simply melt under your fingers.

Playing

You've seen how your kitty behaves when it plays. It likes running up and down, hiding and peeking from around corners, pouncing on everything that moves, and then kicking and biting it "to death." These are all very natural acts for cats to do, both in hunting and playing. When we recreate scenarios in play that cats in the wild encounter when they are hunting, they are in their element and will gleefully play along. They understand that it's just a game and give you playful bites, but sometimes they can get a little too excited or overstimulated and bite down, so be careful not to inadvertently train your furious furball to see your hand as a toy, or else you're in for a world of hurt.

It's a good idea to have playtime right before mealtime, as it has a natural progression to it. In the wild, cats would have an active hunt, followed by their meal, a leisurely groom, and maybe a nap. There's no need to limit playtime to mealtime though, and even a small treat after an exhausting round of play will serve as a great motivator to get active. A quick tickle of the tummy, but only for a moment and no longer, can instigate a bout of play, as will hiding around a corner, or other cues your cat associates with fun.

Playing and interacting with them strengthens the bond between you and your cat. Playing not only keeps cats active but there is evidence that cats who have more stimulation when playing are sick less often. It's also therapeutic for cat parents watching the hilarity thus improving mood.

Toys and Games

Cats like to play a variety of games that either involve natural intuition or can be trained to play more difficult games with simple rules. As long as they enjoy the game and it's not too complex, they will remain interested. Most cats like the chase part of playing fetch as much as dogs do, but rarely do they bring it back. Kitty Fishing Poles take care of the return trip for you both.

Hide and seek is one of the more natural ways of playing with your cat. They are naturally inquisitive and will readily play along, unless they are sleeping, or just not in the mood. Go somewhere in the house where your cat isn't, then call them. When they come and find you, you can reward them. It's one of the most passive ways to play and can literally be done sitting down. Another way to play is by scratching under a blanket or on the side of a box with your hand. Once they jump in or out to find your hand, you can give them praise.

There are a multitude of cat toys on the market for interactive play. Just make sure the material is safe for them to play with and if there is a possibility of your cat chewing off and swallowing pieces, either avoid the toy entirely or only allow them to play with it while being supervised.

Cats lose interest in their toys relatively quickly so don't leave them lying around for too long, but circulate them with other toys every so often. Here are a few good examples of toys cats enjoy playing with.

- Balls are a classic toy.
- Cat teaser toys or wands work well.

- Kickers or soft plushies. They're definitely the most roughly treated cat item after the scratching post, and they must be able to withstand powerful clawed kicks, aggressive bites, and being batted back and forth across the floor.

- Cat-safe laser pointers. Not all lasers are created equal, make sure to only use lasers that are safe for your cat's eyes, to prevent damage even blindness. Lasers must never be pointed at highly reflective surfaces, since the reflected beam can still be dangerous. A never-ending chase can leave your cat frustrated. End every laser session with a victory, like pointing the elusive dot on a physical toy, or on a treat so it can be "caught".

- Cloth bags or refillable catnip plushies.

For a bit of solo play, try puzzle feeders. Different types of puzzle feeders provide varying levels of difficulty to stimulate your clever feline's mind and kick the boredom.

Don't worry too much about commercial toys if what's available on the market doesn't agree with you or is a bit expensive. Cats can have very particular tastes and forking out a lot of money on a toy your cat might not even give a second glance isn't fun. Fortunately, cats are cheap dates, and you can have a ton of fun together by turning some regular household objects into the best toys under the sun.

- Paper balls.
- Paper bags.

- Empty toilet rolls. Sometimes cats love batting them around, but you can make it more appealing by folding the ends in, making a small hole in the side, and filling it with some food pellets, treats, or catnip. It will then automatically dispense some of what's inside as Kitty bats it around.

- Cardboard boxes. If the cat fits, it sits. Granted, not the most exciting toy, but cats do love them, and giving it a few paw-sized holes in the side and popping a favorite toy inside it instantly becomes more exciting.

- A balled-up sock laced with some catnip is a lovely way to recycle a sock that's lost its partner.

- Feathers. Clean and pest-free. Once the shaft shows signs of wear, dispose of it, as sharp bits can start breaking off and might accidentally get ingested.

- Thick cotton string, twine, or rope, to chase and pounce on these as you drag them around.

Speaking Softly

Cats are skittish creatures and loud or unfamiliar noises easily scare them. That includes the voice they've come to know and love. The tone in which you speak can decide the quality of your interaction. It doesn't need to be baby talk, but pet-directed speech (PDS) is a good way of letting your cat know that you are talking to it. When using PDS your voice tends to be slower, softer, and more sing-songy with a higher pitch. Since cats don't have the vocabulary we humans do, we repeat their names or keywords often, including short phrases, like "You hungry?", "Come here", and "Good boy/girl."

Studies have even found that we intone our voices differently and subconsciously depending on the activity we are engaged in. They also show that women are more likely than men to use PDS, probably due to maternal, nurturing instinct and a higher vocal pitch.

Like most animals, non-vocal loud sounds such as firecrackers, honking horns, and construction can be frightening. Try a soothing sound machine melody to reduce the impact of the anxiety-producing noises if they are prolonged.

Good Food

Dogs eat. Cats dine. –Ann Taylor

As obligate carnivores, cats don't have the option to go vegetarian. As mentioned before, cats can't metabolize sugars and carbs well either. That doesn't stop some pet food companies from mixing cheaper additives like corn, among other things, into the cat food they produce to save money on production costs. What's worse is that low-quality food like this could easily lead to feline obesity, diabetes, kidney disease to name a few.

Love your cat by giving it quality, vet-approved food. An occasional treat such as the ones that help reduce tooth plaque is a good idea. Even a tiny amount of the type of grains, fruits, and veggies found in prey stomachs are okay but make sure that meat protein is first on the ingredient list and avoid by-products and fillers. If grain comes before the meat protein, it's not a good quality for your cat. Some greens are okay such as the oat grass some pet stores sell.

Grains like brown rice, corn, couscous, oats, greens like asparagus, broccoli, carrot, peas, and fruit like peeled and deseeded apples and watermelon, banana, blueberries, cantaloupe, and pumpkin are all safe for cats to eat. These foods make up a tiny portion of feral cat diets given how small their prey's stomachs are, even if full. Given a choice, they usually won't choose them or thank you for reducing their meat in favor of those upscale blends now on the market. If a cat likes it, that's most important, so don't force it, thinking you're doing them a favor. The only additive to cat food needed is taurine. In the USA, taurine is required in cat food but because it is destroyed in processing, it has to be added afterwards.

Clean Litter Box

Cats simply hate a dirty litter box, even more than you do. They have to climb in there, and won't appreciate getting dirty litter between their toes. Scented litter won't hide a dirty litter box from your cat, their noses are far too well developed to let it slide. Scoop the poop at least once a day, and replace all the litter once a week.

Strolling

Cats long to be outside but it's dangerous, especially in cities with many vehicles or areas with lots of predators such as coyotes, foxes, wolves, owls, hawks, eagles, and many others. While many cats will refuse to be walked, some will adjust to harness and leash if you allow them to lead. If not, there are great strollers on the market for pets. This is a real treat for indoor cats to be in your company and outdoors and it's a good idea to familiarize your cat with the neighborhood in case they should get out so they can find their way home.

Even if you are not in the mood or the weather is not great, your cat will still enjoy sitting outside on the porch or balcony in the fresh air, watching life go by, as long as it is not raining.

How Cats Worship Their

Human Slaves

A cat has absolute emotional honesty: human beings, for one reason or another, may hide their feelings, but a cat does not. –
Ernest Hemingway

Touching

It might look like your cat is smiling when you stroke it, but it is likely just a projection of our own feelings. Though cats do have muscles in their faces that can give them expressions, cats "smile" by slow blinking.

Kneading, also known as "making biscuits", "making muffins", or "happy paws" is when a cat rhythmically pushes the pads of its paws while flexing its toes and claws into a soft surface, reminiscent of a baker kneading some dough. It's one of the first actions kittens engage in when they nurse and serves the function of stimulating milk flow and production from their mom. As this is an intimate familial bonding ritual it should be encouraged (It's also adorable). Often cats will make biscuits all on their own, purring contentedly while kneading a soft surface of their choice which includes other cats, but they might also choose to knead on your lap, your stomach, or your chest. It's one way of showing you that they are comfortable and happy to be in your presence. Some cats twitch their legs or pelvis while they knead and may enjoy being petted, but it's a matter of style and preference. Praise them while they are at it.

Cats have sweat and scent glands in their paws and leave their scent when they scratch trees, furniture, or scratching posts, so they might be kneading as an excuse to claim you or the blanky as their own.

Some have attributed kneading to nesting behavior inherited from their ancestors who might have engaged in actions like tamping down their bedding to make it comfortable before curling up, as cats today often knead a surface before settling down for a good nap.

Grooming you with sandpaper kisses is a cat's way of showing you affection and while in the process of licking you, it may even get a little playful and grab hold of you. A firm "no" from you usually gets the point across if they get a little rough, and they will likely stop nibbling and continue grooming. Cats routinely engage in mutual grooming among themselves as a way of showing acceptance and affection. If those sandpaper kisses become too much, gently disengage, as it is an important bonding ritual that shouldn't be punished but rather encouraged. Then distract the cat with play or another activity.

Judging by how many times your cat has tripped you when rubbing up against your legs, you would be remiss in thinking that your cat is plotting your murder. It is actually showing you affection.

A cat's head butt and head rubbing are called bunting. They bunt a range of objects and other animals, including you. It serves as stimulation for the cat and depending on the context in which they engage in this behavior, might indicate pleasure, claiming ownership, or showing affection. It is undoubtedly affectionate if it happens spontaneously, but if it's happening around mealtime Kitty might just be buttering you up.

Cats have scent glands at the corners of their mouths, under their chins, at their temples, along their tails, and under the aforementioned paws, and they will often rub against objects as a means to spread their scent around their territory. You will notice that when your cat engages in this behavior it will likely curl its tail around your leg, like a monkey's around a branch, usually accompanied by an admiring gaze up at you.

Purring

As mentioned earlier in the section on Purr creation, a cat usually purrs when it is relaxed and content, but if it is at rest in your lap and purring it can only mean love. Your cat is telling you that it feels safe and calm enough to let its guard down around you, and for the usually stealthy predator to start its little engine up, you must be exceptionally trustworthy.

Playing

A kitten is the most irresistible comedian in the world. –Agnes Repplier

When a cat throws itself down at your feet and rolls around, it's an invitation to come over. Even when they scoot away just as you stoop to pet them, they still want you to pursue them. This playful behavior is one of their ways of communicating that they want your attention and will enjoy playing with you. Cats behave this way only with the most trusted cats and humans in their inner circle.

Cats may even hide around corners when they hear you coming and pounce on you as you approach. If they catch you unawares, try not to make a fuss as it might frighten them. They will appreciate it if you give chase, or praise and give them attention.

The occasional stray item (seen as a toy to your cat) on your desk or table, whether it has any business lying there or not, may fall prey to your feline's curiosity and will soon be experiencing a quick trip to the floor and the hereafter, that is, under the couch or cupboard never to be seen again, or until the next spring clean. Maybe your cat knows the location of every one of your socks that's gone missing?

Proximity

Though cats are solitary creatures, they don't want to be alone all the time. They need social interaction and will seek their humans out. It's partially because they feel safe and they enjoy having you around, but they are also curious creatures by nature. They want to be nearby to see what you are up to. When the human isn't quite as entertaining as they had hoped, they will stick around and sleep somewhere nearby, or snuggle up when we go to bed. Cats are naturally nocturnal and therefore most active at night, so it speaks volumes if they prefer to lie down and sleep with you instead.

On occasion, you might find yourself hard at work with a book, hobby, or keyboard, only to have your favorite feline plop itself down right in front of you with complete disregard for what you were doing. They're astute observers of where your focus is, and when you've not tended to them for a while. they take it into their own paws to save their human from their drudgery. Even when they type all sorts of nonsense with their backsides on a keyboard, create abstract paw print art on your sketchpad, or decide to nibble on an unplaced puzzle piece, they just want you to be with them.

Talking Back

If cats could talk, they wouldn't. —Nan Porter

Kittens meow to their mother, but they grow out of it. Adult cats rarely, if ever, meow at another cat, reserving their meow almost exclusively for communicating with humans. Your cat will meow back at whatever nonsense you say to it. The fact that you are even talking to them is enough, but it's your tone that elicits a response. Not unlike us, cats have preferences when it comes to who they feel like talking to, and will usually only do so with their loved ones or possibly if nervous with a new person almost like asking for reassurance.

Traditionally, cats were considered to only have 12 vocalizations, but in 2019, a research paper by A. Shojai, suggested that cats have an impressive repertoire of 21 and more vocalizations. They may use any number of them on a daily basis and they all convey slightly different messages. Different environments, moods, or other things might influence how they intone some meows. Research into cat vocalizations is only just beginning to shed light on how widely cats are able to communicate. Some of the previous discussion of sounds in the chapter on cat parts is relevant here. The softer, closed-mouth sounds of purring, chirps, and such are expressions to their human of contentment, acknowledgment, and agreement. The louder open-mouth meow sounds are asking for your attention. Attention to what is for you to figure out.

Vulnerability

Showing you their bellies is another way of showing you that they trust you. Exposing their most vulnerable spots is something they only reserve for the most loved and trusted of humans. This might seem like they are extending an invitation for you to rub their bellies, but be warned: not all cats are comfortable with having their bellies touched, or they might be too excited to allow it. If the need overcomes you and you simply must risk life and limb, do so slowly and softly. A reflexive twitch from them is usually the sign to back off. Just like some of us are ticklish, they can be ticklish too, and when they are, their claws will come out.

When your beloved cat approaches you with its tail up, it is a friendly greeting to you, but then Kitty jumps in your lap or walks across the table past you only to turn its butt toward you. What's going on here?

It's a true, albeit strange sign of affection. Cats will often lift their tails to other familiar cats to signal that they are not a threat and to offer them a sniff. You are by no means obligated to take them up on the offer. Turning the other cheek, so to speak, is a courtesy reserved only for their trusted inner circle. It's akin to our way of -ahem- kissing a friend's cheek. Like their bellies, a cat's behind is vulnerable, and their choice to display it to you shows trust and friendship.

Choosing You

Cats will often forgo their favorite sleeping spot by coming to lie close to you. They might follow you around or leave the room they were comfortably napping in if they notice that you got up. Actively seeking you out shows you that they enjoy your company and will choose to interact with you in lieu of other comforts, like toys, scents, and even food, according to a study done at Oregon State University.

Gifts

Outside cats will often bring home their catch and announce their arrival with a distinct meow. It's more than simply bragging about how great a hunter it is, it's your cat telling you that it cares about you enough to call you over to come and share in its bounty. As gruesome as the sight of a recently mauled bird, mouse, lizard or other small creature is, believe it or not, it is a gift. Putting our feelings aside for the unfortunate wretch that crossed your cat's path, it is something to praise your cat for. After all, it is sharing with family.

There is a common misconception that cats behave like this because they think we cannot hunt for ourselves. A mother cat will bring prey back to her den, often alive, to wean kittens off of her milk and teach them how to hunt and kill, but the same scenario is not applicable to us. Our cats most definitely know that we are the food providers and the distinction between store-bought food and freshly caught prey is lost on them.

Feline Faux Paws that Make Your Cat Cantankerous

Loud Noises

Cats are the ultimate connoisseurs of quiet and take great pride in their ability to tiptoe around in silence. They spend the vast majority of their lives stealthily slinking around the house without so much as a peep, so when a loud noise interrupts their peaceful existence, they can make quite a fuss.

A cat's hearing is far more sensitive than ours, as witnessed when their little ears twitch or perk up at a sound we don't hear. Being alert is a 24/7 job for them, so cats startle easily. They not only have an instinctive response to loud noises that might mean danger but also a reflexive response that happens in 20 milliseconds or less, so fast that cats can't even think about what's happening before their bodies and limbs stiffen up and send them flying into the air. A human's reflex is typically 3–10 times slower.

It takes our little masters of stealth longer to recognize our voices than their reflex response allows, so even a familiar voice raised suddenly and unexpectedly could have them running in fright.

Rough Handling

Being independent creatures, cats value their personal space and the freedom to move about untouched. Handling a cat roughly can be uncomfortable and even painful for them, which is why they may show signs of distress, aggression, or fear when being handled in such a way.

Cats are built differently from dogs and humans. They have thinner skin and a more fragile bone structure. Rough handling, like tail pulling, grabbing, or squeezing, can easily cause potential injuries or bruises.

Being handled roughly will cause anxiety, overwhelm, and feeling threatened, and cause a negative association with the person handling it. It may perceive the person as a threat, and the cat's instinct to defend itself could result in lashing out and scratching or biting the handler. It will result in a damaged relationship between the cat and human, which could take time and patience to repair.

Young children can be very rough with pets and should be taught great empathy for animals. Teach them how to handle cats correctly, especially delicate kittens. By teaching gentle handling and respect for a cat's boundaries, you can help kindle a positive and safe relationship between your child and your fur baby, but it will require patience and supervision.

- Teach them never to pull or tug on a cat's tail or ears. Show the child how to stroke the cat's fur and use slow movements, putting emphasis on lightly stroking with the grain.

- Always supervise while the child interacts with the cat, during the early stages of learning. Make sure the child understands that the cat is a living creature with needs and feelings just like they have and that they must treat them with great care and respect.

- Teach the child that they must respect the cat's boundaries and how to recognize when the cat has had enough and wants to be left alone. Show them when cats aren't in the mood to play or be handled, and how to tell from the cat's body language when they must avoid unwanted interactions or they might scare the cat and get hurt themselves.

- Make clear rules for the child on what is the right way to interact with the cat and what is the wrong way, like not picking them up without permission, not disturbing them when they are sleeping, and not playing rough.

- Encourage the child to develop empathy towards the cat by talking to them about the cat's needs, feelings, and behaviors.

Uninvited Belly Rubs

The most vulnerable cat parts must be respected. Some cats don't mind belly rubs and might invite just about anyone in for a rub, but most cats don't trust quite as easily. As the belly is a sensitive area, they might even deny access to their most trusted humans.

When cats expose their bellies, it doesn't mean they will allow you to touch them, but rather extend your hand toward them and offer a chin scratch that goes progressively lower before diving in belly-first if no signal to stop occurs.

Too Much of Anything

Domestic cats usually enjoy being petted and brushed, but all good things come to an end. When a cat is overstimulated, it will tell you in a variety of ways.

Strike one: the first and most likely response to unwanted petting would be a firm paw pushing your hand away or a swat at the offending hand, nails optional.

Strike two: a threatening hiss, a growl, ears pulled back, or a tail whipping back and forth. It ought to be abundantly clear by now that they have had enough.

Strike three: the teeth come out: if the human still doesn't get the picture the teeth and nails come out, maybe even a bunny kick or two. Can't say it's undeserved.

They can want you to stop for a variety of reasons; if the petting or brushing is too much, too rough, or is in a sensitive, irritated, or injured area; if it's by someone they don't trust, or they might just not want petting anymore. It's a cat's prerogative.

Dirty Litter Box

You know that feeling when nature calls and you enter a public restroom, but there is absolutely no way that you will use the facilities? Cats feel the same about a dirty litter box. Particularly if it's a litter box they have to share with other cats.

Cats originally evolved to help them survive in arid desert environments. As a result, their kidneys adapted to concentrate urine so not much water is wasted when they urinate. As their diet is carnivorous, their urine also contains a lot of fat, which makes the smell linger. The combination of these two features makes quite a pungent mix. Their waste and smell quickly accumulate and make using a dirty box unbearable. Not only will the strong odor of ammonia sting their eyes and noses, but the wetness of the litter will deter them as well. This will force them to seek out other areas to conduct their business. In multi-cat households, other cats might take it up as a competition, and try to cover the scent of urine with their own brand.

The minimum daily scooping can be a pain, but not nearly as much as having to clean up a mess made outside the litter box. It could lead to a nightmare cycle of bad habits being formed. The high-fat content in a cat's urine can make it particularly difficult to clean, with some household chemicals like ammonia-based cleaners making the problem even worse.

Decontaminate the crime scene and use enzymatic soaps and surgical spirit to clean the area and make sure to leave no evidence. If the smell is not completely eliminated, your cat might think it's okay to return to the scene of the crime.

A dirty litter box might not be the only thing causing your cat to choose a more suitable spot to drop a deuce. A new litter box or a new type of litter is a change (something cats don't like), so it's advised to inaugurate a new litter box or litter with a little bit of the old litter. They'll get the idea. Observe them until the habit is established.

Other factors to consider that might cause a change in their toilet routine include your cat's age or other health issues, changes to the inside environment, like new pets, babies, children, renovations, and visitors, or elements of the outside environment changing, like rainy, snowy, or cold weather, construction, harassment from neighborhood cats or animals, or accidentally blocking off access to the litter box.

Getting Wet

To bathe a cat takes brute force, perseverance, courage of conviction—and a cat. The last ingredient is usually hardest to come by. –Stephen Baker

While there are exceptions, for most cats getting wet is horrible. Even dripping condensation from a glass onto the fur ball in your lap may cause outrage and immediate departure from said lap. That doesn't mean they aren't curious about water as many a cat parent can relate to the odd appearance of their cat kids on the edge of the tub while they are bathing. No, they are not trying to see you naked, they are likely trying to figure out why in hell you are submerged in water and or what is that foamy stuff all over you. Let one slip into the tub and watch out! If you escape without a puncture wound, feel lucky.

Change...any Change

Cats are habitual creatures, and curious too, so any changes that you make around the house will not go unnoticed for long.

The experiences cats have in their kittenhood can have a lifelong effect on how they cope with changes. When exposed to changes in a positive way early on in life, cats tend to be less fearful and more capable of dealing with changes in their lives when they come up at a later stage.

Cats need to be socialized as early as five to six weeks of age, which means the breeder or shelter you adopt your kitten from needs to do the hard work, which they most likely did not. But never fear, cats are nothing if not adaptable. The sooner you start their socialization the better. Start out small, and introduce your kitten to more people than just the family it will be living with. Have them pick it up, play with it, and feed it. Consider what daily noises your kitten will be experiencing, like the TV, an instrument, the vacuum cleaner, or a hair dryer, and get it used to the noises.

Sometimes these changes are out of your control, like the death of a pet or family member. Cats are known to grieve too, and it is important to still give them positive attention and praise. Sometimes in cases like these, including extreme changes to their living conditions or extremely frightening experiences, natural anti-anxiety options like Bach Flower Remedy drops (for pets) in water or pheromone emitters/sprays, and vet-approved drugs may be useful as short-term solutions, although a lot of older cats don't respond well to medications. It's best to consult a vet to discuss your options or alternatives to treatment.

When changes are in your control, it is a good idea to plan ahead to make the transition as smooth as possible for yourself and your cat. Make changes gradually and give your cat enough time to notice that something is afoot, but have plenty of familiar items and smells around to reassure it. Your cat might become stressed at this point, so observe its behavior closely and if you notice anything out of the ordinary, such as a change in its grooming or litter box routine, a loss of appetite, or apprehensive behavior, stop changing things and reverse a step or two, if possible, until things are normal again.

Here are a few things you can do to help your cats deal with change:

- Provide an escape route, a safe, quiet haven on top of a wardrobe or cabinet that it has easy access to so it can retreat if it feels overwhelmed. If at all possible, give your cat a vantage point so it can see what's going on, but still feel safe and secure. Don't make your cat's haven on the ground where it won't feel safe even if it's hidden, especially if the change is a new dog that might harm or harass it.

- Give your cat easy access to water and food that is out of the dog's reach and provide an accessible litter box, preferably somewhere quiet or in a separate room.

- Give it enough attention, so it won't feel neglected or abandoned.

- Use products that help calm your cat down, such as anxiety relief vests or wraps, pheromonal sprays or collars, and vet-approved medications.

Home Invasions of New Creatures

We know that our furballs are going to balk at the idea of change. Their territory, routine, and general dominance over us have been nurtured to a point where predictability is our furry friends' existence. If you do plan on introducing any new pets, love interests, roommates, or family members, there are ways to do this considerately and kindly to reduce your cat's stress reaction.

Introducing a New Cat

With the introduction of a new feline friend that will roam the house freely alongside your resident cat, it is a good idea to keep the new arrival in a separate room in the beginning. Your cat will have noticed right away that there are new scents around, so occasionally have your cat smell a toy or piece of bedding that bears the smell of the new cat, and vice versa, all the while giving them positive attention.

After a few days introduce them face-to-face through a screen door or mesh. Don't hold or restrain your cat to avoid making them feel trapped and anxious. Give them the freedom to move closer and explore without being able to reach one another. Few cats are immediately accepting of a new friend, so expect a few hisses and spits. Give them lots of positive attention and speak gently to them. Once they are over the initial shock of seeing each other, try to have them play separately so they can watch each other. Continue this for a few days until they no longer vocalize when they approach one another through the partition. Be patient with them and let them take their time to get used to one another's presence. The last thing you want to do is introduce them too fast and risk them having a negative experience.

The time has come for a friendly playdate. Close all doors and windows before removing the partition. Keep some treats and toys ready as they can be good icebreakers to take the edge off a stressful situation. Have them play together but be on alert in case things go badly. Once they have played a little and relaxed again, remain in their company for a while, before retiring your pets to their separate rooms again. After another playdate or two with no incident, it should be safe to trust them in each other's company.

Introducing a New Baby

I'm pretty sure your new baby is not news to you, and it shouldn't be for your cat either. Help it prepare for your new bundle of joy with the following tips:

- Have the home setup for the baby prepared well in advance so your cat can investigate the cradle and the new smells of baby products.

- Before your baby is born, your cat should, if possible, have an interaction with a baby human. A baby's cries can be jarring and frightening to a cat that has never heard it before, especially since some baby sounds are eerily similar to cats in distress.

- Don't change your cat's routine. It's not always possible with a newborn to take care of as well, but try to keep things as normal as possible. Give your cat food at the usual time and if there's playtime involved, try to fit it in as well and give it plenty of attention, so it won't feel neglected.

- There's an old wives' tale that cats smother newborns. It hails from the 17th century when sudden infant death syndrome (SIDS) was unknown. Cats are not malicious or vindictive, and although it's theoretically possible that a cat can snuggle up a little too close to your warm little one and hinder its breathing, there have been less than a handful of credible cases of it ever leading to a health issue. Make sure your cat interacts with your baby so they can bond.

Introducing a New Partner

I am not a cat man, but a dog man, and all felines can tell this at a glance—a sharp, vindictive glance. –James Thurber

Cats are smart creatures and although a new resident in the house can be unfamiliar, they'll warm up to anyone who is consistently friendly.

Here are a few tips to speed up the process of making friends:

- Wear clothing from your new partner, or introduce their smell through a strategically placed item of clothing so it can become familiar with the smell.

- Play or pet your cat while wearing the item of clothing, so it can learn to associate the new scent with positive emotions.

- Before your partner comes over, ask them not to wear strong perfume or cologne that can interfere with the introduction. It's been all about scent so far, best not to overdo it.

- Have them sit down or crouch low next to your cat, so the cat doesn't perceive it as threatening if they loom or hover over it.

- Don't force an interaction, like having them pick it up, but let your cat go to them. If it doesn't happen naturally, have them offer it a treat, food, or some catnip.

- Have them speak to your cat in a soft, kindly manner.
- Have them try slow-blinking at your cat.
- Let them play with your cat using some of its favorite toys.

In time your cat will see them as a companion. It's important not to change your cat's routine at this point and to still give it the lion's share of your attention, it was there first, after all, and jealousy is not an unknown emotion to cats.

Travel

There are entire books about traveling with a cat, so this section only hits the highlights and suggests where some additional research is required.

Being Caged

The most important step to make any extended time your cat will be spending caged less stressful is to get a carrier your pussy cat likes and let them be in it as often as they like before your trip. Providing a favorite toy will be comforting, and a piece of your clothing to accompany your cat will be a constant connection to you and your home.

Practice traveling to other destinations your cat might like so your furball won't learn to associate the carrier with negative experiences. In time, your cat will become less and less stressed with being cooped up for a while. Use a treat for positive reinforcement once the journey has come to an end. A light at the end of the tunnel is always good motivation.

Being Medicated

Cats respond to being medicated in a variety of ways, but being a little loopy from medication is a scary experience that makes your cat feel like it's not in control. Not all cats react to medications the same way. Before traveling the first time, when you think medication will be needed, try out medication options to make sure it works as desired. Do this some weeks before your trip in case more than one medication proves to be unacceptable so you'll have enough time to find the right one.

After the trip, don't allow your cat to roam in a hazy medicated state that might cause injury. Their mobility and ability to perceive threats will be far from perfect. The best way to deal with a drugged-up Kitty is to make sure it's in a quiet environment where it can safely sleep it off. Close the windows, and if necessary, the door, but give it access to a comfy place to lie down, food, water, and a litter box. You can give it a treat once it feels better.

By Car

Most cats don't regularly ride in cars and when they do, most don't have past positive associations. A ride in the car usually involves a trip to the veterinarian, a boarding kennel, or a groomer. It's like a blaring alarm to them. The older the cat, the higher their level of anxiety, having experienced many more unpleasant trips. It is thought that if cats are exposed to car travel from an early age, they can become more comfortable with it, and if these experiences turn out not to be scary most of the time, their anxiety will be less, even as they age.

Invest in a good carrier for trips. They're also great for a drive to the vet's office. It's not safe for a cat to be outside of the carrier in the car. Just like seat belts are there for a reason, the carrier is there to protect them in case of an accident. Your cat might also slip out the door or window, or get spooked and run off if not in the carrier.

By Air

Traveling by air with a cat is complex because it differs by the airline, by the country you are entering, if international, and whether or not the cat will be in the cabin or cargo. It can be further complicated, not to mention riskier for cats in cargo, if you must make a connection. There is just too much to summarize all the research you need to do before considering an airplane trip for your cat.

From experience, air travel is extra stressful for your cat and you with both the trip to the airport and the flight, let alone the crowds of people. After several experiences both domestic and international, if cats were meant to fly, they would have wings seems an appropriate sentiment.

No matter where or what airline, you must have documentation and meet airline-specific requirements, and it will differ if the cat goes cargo (only if absolutely no choice) or in the cabin. That means advanced planning is essential.

The following are a few tips to help lessen your stress about flying with your fur baby so you can focus on preparing it for the ordeal:

- Choose an airline with a good track record for transporting pets.

- Keep all the relevant documentation for you and your cat on your person, including a photo of you and your pet, and vet records just in case you get separated.

- Book a direct flight to your destination to avoid the risks involved with connecting flights, flight delays, long layovers, and missed connections.

- Feed your cat within four hours of checking in, but not within four hours before the departure time. If you live a couple of hours from an airport, you're already in trouble.

- Don't travel with your pet during peak holiday times.

- Have your cat microchipped and put a collar on it with an ID tag clearly displaying your name and number clearly.

- Usually, airline policy is one pet per carrier per person per cabin section so book way in advance to get them in the cabin with you.

- Use some pheromonal spray on the airline carrier and put a pheromonal collar on your cat.

- Wrap your cat in a Thundershirt, a calming vest that applies constant gentle pressure that's similar to swaddling a baby. It is vet-recommended as an alternative to or in addition to medicating your cat, and it's proven to reduce anxiety, fear, and over-excitement.

- Never leave your cat unattended.

- It really has to be an emergency to put your beloved in the cargo hold with all the horror stories of mishandling and loss that pepper the news. Perhaps consider alternative airlines and **never** check your cat if it's a connecting flight unless you really like gambling. The odds are in your favor but bad things do happen. They are often treated like baggage despite the "Live Animal" stickers on the carrier.

It's not a good idea to be traveling with a cat that has known medical problems, especially respiratory issues, even if it accompanies you in the cabin. Because of the inherent risks involved, some airlines will not transport brachycephalic, snub-nosed, cats. Your flat-faced British or American Shorthair, Persian, Himalayan, and Burmese are but a few of the more popular breeds not allowed on commercial flights.

Needless to say, taking Kitty on an adventure with you is quite expensive. International customs, import, and quarantine fees can be mind-boggling and a quarantine period may be too long to be viable depending on your trip length. If moving, there is no choice.

If all of the above is giving you heart palpitations, why not consider hiring a pet transport company if you are moving overseas to take care of some of the legwork for you? These trained professionals won't be cheap, but they know just how much your pet means to you and will do their utmost to ensure that your cat arrives safely at its destination. It's much better for the cat to stay with a sitter if your trip is shorter.

Vet Visits

As little as we enjoy going to a doctor to be probed and prodded, your cat likes it even less. Occasional vet visits needn't be overly stressful if you properly familiarize your cat with its carrier as described in the section "Being Caged" including the familiar toy or clothing item to calm your cat somewhat. A treat or two during and after the visit can help calm them and provide positive reinforcement.

Schedule a visit ahead of time and try to plan accordingly so you can avoid spending unnecessary time in the waiting area, the sooner it's done the better. Keep a folder of your cat's medical records. Since vets do not have the interconnectivity of medical records like human medical offices, this is the cat parent's responsibility. It comes in handy if traveling and the cat needs to go to a new vet at your destination for whatever reason. Partnering with your regular vet to provide the best care includes knowing when shots are due and how long it has been since dental care has been done, especially in older cats. Review their last couple of vet visit summaries before you go.

It's not always possible, as in an emergency, but have your carrier ready to grab and go at the drop of a hat. Your cat might have to stay overnight in the kennel, so make sure to provide it with all the creature comforts it might need. Vets will also have visitation hours in case of an extended stay, so keep your kitty's spirits up by visiting it with treats (if the vet approves) and some familiar company.

Claw Clipping

There is no humor to be found in the practice of declawing. Declawing cats is an inhumane procedure done for the sake of convenience, an attempt to forcefully further domesticate the cat. When considering a cat as a pet, understand that they have an instinctual need to scratch. They can scratch up furniture and hurt your skin, be it during play, as defense, or even just by accident. It's all part of having a cat. A healthy cat includes claws. With some patience, love, and consistent signals, there are many ways to reduce and even eliminate the destruction their claws can cause, short of cutting off parts of the cat.

Unlike our nails, a cat's claw is firmly attached to the bone. Its removal involves cutting out the toe bones that claws grow from, that is, surgical amputation of the last joint of a cat's toes. That would be the equivalent of a human having the last joint of their fingers and toes amputated. It can lead to chronic paw pain, back pain, tissue death, lameness, infection, soiling themselves or soiling outside the litter box, increased aggression and biting, and other bad behaviors. If done improperly, the claw can regrow, causing bone spurs and nerve damage. A cat will often hide the pain they feel, an instinctual response to not appear weak and vulnerable, so, to many cat owners, they appear to have fully recovered. Not so.

All this adds up to a lower quality of life for cats, not to mention the denial of instinctual behaviors such as stretching their front legs when scratching their posts and jumping when they cannot grip and falling instead. In time, they will stop jumping and stop being a fully realized cat. They also lose their primary form of defense, so they feel increased vulnerability. Many cats never recover from the trauma, and may have their personalities altered forever.

Sadly, 20–25% of cats in the U.S. have been declawed, and 55% of U.S. cat owners consider the practice acceptable (Little Big Cat). It seems to be a peculiarly American attitude to have a cat declawed for the protection of its human's furnishings and/or skin with nary a thought for the life-long disability of the cat. Outside the U.S., declawing is illegal in forty-two countries and outlawed in eight provinces in Canada. In the U.S. it is outlawed in the states of New York and Maryland, in eight cities in California, also in Allentown, Austin, the City of St. Louis, St. Louis County, Denver, Madison, and Pittsburgh (Alley Cat Allies, 2023).

There are options other than declawing available, like providing them with scratching posts, regularly clipping their nails, using clear furniture protection strips to discourage scratching upholstery, or even using snazzy stick-on vinyl nail caps (see softpaws.com). Cats should be able to live their best lives, with their nails intact. If any of the alternatives to declawing aren't feasible, consider a different pet. Rabbits are a good alternative: they're portable, quiet, cute, soft, cuddly, and can be trained to use a litterbox. They do have small claws but they are only used defensively–the bunny kick or to hold their food up to their mouths.

Because cat paws are very sensitive, grabbing them, and squeezing the toe beans to extend the claws for clipping is something most cats do not like. If you start clipping your cat's claws as a kitten, they may get used to it enough to allow it as an adult. While in kittenhood it's much easier to be gentle.

Claws typically need to be clipped about every six weeks but can vary slightly by cat. As difficult as it is to be gentle when a cat is unhappy, don't give in to impatience, get unnerved, or get angry. Usually, the back paws are more sensitive than the mitten claws. Because of this, you may be able to get a front claw or two clipped when they are drowsing on your lap or next to you before they realize what's happening and over several days get them all. Not so much the back feet.

Most people will need a second pair of arms and hands to get all the nails clipped. Using a towel to wrap around the cat will help prevent panic scratches and stabilize them to make clipping safer for both of you. Above all, squeeze their pads gently but firmly so you can clearly see the claw and look for the pink quick. Cut below the quick just like you would a human fingernail. Proceed with as much authority and speed as you can safely. The cat will pick up on your anxiety and become further panicked so stay calm and confident. Always reward with treats and lavish praise.

Alternatively, you can book an appointment with your vet to get them clipped which will be even more stressful for the cat if they haven't gotten used to car rides and then there is the additional cost. Sometimes you may be able to enlist a vet tech or assistant to come to your home for a fee.

Catifying Your Home

Your house will always be blessed with love, laughter, and friendship if you have a cat. –Lewis Carroll

Cat Angels On High

Cats are natural climbers. It is a fundamental instinct of all cats to climb and seek out high areas, especially if there's a lot of foot traffic from humans and other non-climbing pets on the ground. Cats love to be above it all and survey their kingdom from a position of safety.

Allow your cat access to a windowsill where they can observe the outside world. It's a bit like cat TV. Cats love to watch the comings and goings of things and are avid bird and squirrel watchers. If the windowsill is on the second floor or higher, make sure that they can't get to the outside.

Try a little cat Feng Shui to create some balance in its world. Place furniture with gradual increases in height so your cat can reach the tops of bookcases, high shelves, and valances above windows. Cats like to be able to circumnavigate the room without touching the floor, similar to a childhood game of "the floor is lava". Consider a well-placed mounted shelf or floating shelf to extend their accessible terrain further.

Cat trees are a wonderful idea for extending a cat's vertical limits. Most cat trees incorporate a few extra interactive elements, like scratching posts, toy mounts, cat caves, and hammocks.

More Litter Box

Cats have a highly developed sense of smell and rely heavily on it in their daily routine. The rule of thumb when it comes to litter boxes is that you should have at least one box per cat in the household plus one extra, especially when cats are kept indoors. Cats can get fussy when it comes to litter boxes. Most cats prefer to have a litter box of their own. Other cats might try to show dominance by leaving their waste uncovered, especially when there are other cats in the household, or when neighborhood cats trespass on your cat's territory. Nothing says "stay away" quite like the smell of poop.

Water, Water, Everywhere

Cats may not be overly fond of water on their bodies, but they do require plenty of fresh water to drink. Cats drink an average of two tablespoons or one fluid ounce of water per pound of body weight per day, and even more in the summer. They might drink less water when they are fed wet food.

Never keep their food and water bowls near one another in the same location. Cats are finicky and aren't fond of drinking water when they can smell their food nearby. Double dishes might spill over food to water or vice versa. Not appetizing at all. Multiple water bowls in varied locations are highly recommended.

If you notice that your cat isn't drinking water, consider moving the dish, placing extra dishes of water in other locations, which is always a good idea anyway, changing the type of dish, or trying a cat fountain for running water. Sufficient water is the most important thing you can do that can prevent or delay kidney disease, the most common cat killer. If wet food is part of the diet, add a little extra water to make it porridge-like, but not soup-like. Carefully monitor the situation and if these options don't work consult a vet as soon as possible.

Always provide clean dishes for your cats to drink and eat from, and be sure to rinse off any soapy residue before drying or refilling them.

Scratching Posts

Cats love to scratch. It's one of their most normal, instinctive behaviors and is very necessary, but can be frustrating if it happens to your brand-new leather couch. They can scratch for a variety of reasons, including play, expressing emotions, marking objects with their scent, shedding the outer shell of their nails, and stretching, which is part of the reason cats stay so flexible. Older cats often lose the ability to retract their claws, which can be uncomfortable for them and may impair their ability to walk and jump, especially on carpeted surfaces and other woven materials where their nails could snag. They might need to scratch a lot more than younger cats, or have their nails trimmed more often to provide them with some relief.

Cats like to fully stretch out when they scratch. Posts with a vertical area as tall as the cat is when they stand on their hind legs are perfect. Ensure that it stands firmly and won't wobble when they scratch, as cats like to get a firm grip and have tremendous pulling strength that shouldn't be underestimated. Some cats also like scratching carpets and rugs, so a large flat area to scratch should also do nicely.

Place scratchers around the house strategically, especially near upholstered furniture. The aim is to divert your cat's attention to the preferred item to scratch. Positive reinforcement goes a long way, so praising them and engaging in positive play when they use their scratchers tells them you like that. Try to divert their scratching behavior to the scratching post rather than scold them for scratching the wrong thing. Cats have no concept of right or wrong, so they won't be able to associate scolding with any damage to furniture. They might pick up from your tone of voice that you are unhappy and then run away from you, but it won't stop them from scratching when you're not around. It might also harm your cat's bond with you, perceiving you as unpredictable and causing them some anxiety.

Any new unfamiliar object has an air of mystique for a cat and they will be curious about a new post. They might not immediately know what to do with it or won't feel comfortable using it yet. You can try catnip to attract them to a scratcher. The smell will get them excited and before long they will give it a try. Also, try playing with them around the post using a wand, string, or laser pointer to guide them. They will interact with the scratcher during play and discover that it has a pleasing texture and that there's nothing to be afraid of.

If your cat still prefers scratching where you don't want it to, consider temporarily making these surfaces unappealing. Sticky tape, smooth plastic, or a bed sheet draped over the area won't be near as fun to scratch, and your cat will seek out other spots and likely settle on its scratcher instead. Once the habit of using the scratcher is established you can remove the deterrents.

Conclusion

A happy arrangement: many people prefer cats to other people, and many cats prefer people to other cats. –Mason Cooley

We hope you've smiled and laughed along at all the quirks and antics that our fur babies get up to, from knocking things off tables to sitting on our keyboards while we work, cats definitely keep us on our toes. Would we want it any other way?

We've illustrated conclusively how truly unique cats are. They're independent, curious, and full of purr-sonality. They can be aloof one minute and snuggling up lovingly the next, incredibly agile and graceful one moment, then turn into clumsy goofballs.

We know that our furry friends are more than just pets. They're confidants during tough times, muses to inspire us to do great things, clowns, idols, hunters, companions, but most of all family. We'll do everything to make them happy, even if that means waking up at 3:00 a.m. to fill the food bowl, again.

Your relationship with your cat may be the most complex and satisfying one you ever have or be second only to your closest human relationships.

So, whether you're a longtime cat lover and owner, or you're thinking about adopting a feline companion of your own for the first time, we hope that we prepared you for what's in store and given you a deeper appreciation for these beautiful, mysterious creatures.

About the Author

Born in Kansas, Julie Dirks knew at the young age of four years old that she would eternally be devoted to cats after reading the children's book "Millions of Cats" by Wanda Gág. For the next year, she wished and imagined her first cat, Kitty, who manifested one afternoon on her front porch. While Kitty's life was lost a year later in a ladder accident, several months after, she witnessed a litter of kittens being born and subsequently adopted one of the orange fluffballs, Topaz. She has seldom been without a feline friend since. Julie's life with cats has been a wonderful one full of learning, growing, and making great homes for her feline loves. Her cats have been consolers and comforters in the hard times as well as endlessly entertaining, loving, and fascinating in better times.

Julie's background as an analyst and researcher, her life experience with cats, and her B.A. in English, combined to create *The Entertaining Cat Lovers Guide Understand Your Cat*. Julie, an avid gardener, currently resides with her cat, Cesil, in Western Michigan on the shores of that Great Lake.

References

Alley Cat Allies. (2023). Keep Cats' Claws on Their Paws. Alley Cat Allies. https://www.alleycat.org/take-action/ban-declawing-keep-cats-claws/

Arlington Veterinary Center. (2022, February 18). Abraham Lincoln: Friend to Felines | President's Day at AVC. Arlingtonvet. https://www.arlingtonvet.com/abraham-lincoln-friend-to-felines/

Baker, J. I. (2019). LIFE Cats. Life Books.

Barbash, Y. (2023). Cats, Bastet and the Worship of Feline Gods. ARCE. https://arce.org/resource/cats-bastet-and-worship-feline-gods

Biello, D. (2007, August 16). Strange but True: Cats Cannot Taste Sweets. Scientific American. https://www.scientificamerican.com/article/strange-but-true-cats-cannot-taste-sweets/

Bland, A. (2013, March 20). Is Taking Your Pet on an Airplane Worth the Risk? Smithsonian; Smithsonian.com. https://www.smithsonianmag.com/travel/is-taking-your-pet-on-an-airplane-worth-the-risk-6241533/

Borgi, M., & Cirulli, F. (2016). Pet Face: Mechanisms Underlying Human-Animal Relationships. Frontiers in Psychology, 7. https://doi.org/10.3389/fpsyg.2016.00298

Bravecto. (2021, April 20). Why Do Cats Purr and How to Learn What Your Cat Is Saying. Bravecto Blog. https://blog.bravecto.co.za/cats/why-do-cats-purr-and-how-learn-what-your-cat-is-saying/?gclid=Cj0KCQjwlumhBhClARIsABO6 p-zVbGzZ0VBYmKSjBZbieBknVS0-MQv5RrC-lTHm9MPI9Yquxp-WiJEaAlP2EALw_wcB

Breyer, M. (2023, March 19). 10 Things You Didn't Know About Cat Whiskers. Treehugger. https://www.treehugger.com/things-you-didnt-know-about-cat-whiskers-4864051

Broad, M. (2019, January 24). Cat Nose Leather – PoC. Pictures-of-Cats. https://pictures-of-cats.org/cat-nose-leather.html

Bukowski, J. (2018). Ear Structure and Function in Cats. Veterinary Manual; MSD Veterinary Manual. https://www.msdvetmanual.com/cat-owners/ear-disorders-of-cats/ear-structure-and-function-in-cats

Calderone, J. (2018, June 30). Here's Why Cats Have Such Strange, Haunting Eyes, Explained by Science. ScienceAlert. https://www.sciencealert.com/here-s-why-cats-have-such-weird-eyes

Catster. (2020, June 8). Why Does My Cat's Nose Change Color? Catster.

https://www.catster.com/cat-health-care/cats-nose-change-color

Celebrity Pets. (2023). Ian Somerhalder and all about their pets. Celebrity Pets. https://celebritypets.net/pets/ian-somerhalder-pets/

Cerciello, S. (2016). Clinical applications of vibration therapy in orthopaedic practice. Muscles, Ligaments and Tendons Journal. https://doi.org/10.11138/mltj/2016.6.1.147

Chewy Editorial. (2019, December 6). Which Plants Are Poisonous to Cats? A Complete Guide. BeChewy. https://be.chewy.com/which-plants-are-poisonous-to-cats-a-complete-guide/

Church & Dwight Co., Inc. (2019). Your Amazing Cat: How They Jump High & Run Fast | ARM & HAMMER™ Cat Litter. Www.armandhammer.com. https://www.armandhammer.com/articles/how-cats-jump-high-run-fast

Cofflard, M. (2019, June 19). Corsica's "cat-fox": On the trail of what may be a new species. Phys.org. https://phys.org/news/2019-06-corsica-cat-fox-trail-species.html

College Manor Veterinary Hospital. (2018, August 14). 5 Ways to Prevent Your Cat from Scratching Your Furniture. College Manor Veterinary Hospital. https://www.collegemanorvet.com/5-ways-prevent-cat-scratching-furniture/

Cosgrove, N. (2021, December 3). 15 Cat Statistics All Pet Lovers Should Know in 2023. Pet Keen. https://petkeen.com/cat-statistics/#2_32_of_cat_owners_in_2022_are_millennials

Cosgrove, N. (2022, October 7). Do Cats Have Eyebrows? Does it Vary by Breed? Pet Keen. https://petkeen.com/do-cats-have-eyebrows

Cvetkovska, L. (2020, July 10). 60 Peculiar Cat Statistics That Are the Cat's Meow! Petpedia. https://petpedia.co/cat-statistics/

Dempsey, C. (2023, February 3). Why are Cats Flexible? Explore Cats. https://www.explorecats.com/cats-flexible/

Dicke, U., & Roth, G. (2016). Neuronal factors determining high intelligence. Philosophical Transactions of the Royal Society B: Biological Sciences, 371(1685), 20150180. https://doi.org/10.1098/rstb.2015.0180

Digital, T. (2021, June 23). 7 Surprising Facts You Never Knew About Cats. Care First Animal Hospital. https://www.carefirstanimalhospital.com/news-events/7-surprising-facts-you-never-knew-about-cats/

Driscoll, C. A., Clutton-Brock, J., Kitchener, A. C., & O'Brien, S. J. (2009). The Taming of the Cat. Scientific American, 300(6), 68–75. https://doi.org/10.1038/scientificamerican0609-68

Driscoll, C. A., Clutton-Brock, J., Kitchener, A. C., & O'Brien, S. J. (2015). How House Cats Evolved. Scientific American. https://doi.org/10.1038/scientificamericanpets0915-62

Drusus, L. (2017, June 4). 10 of History's Craziest Cat People. Mental Floss. https://www.mentalfloss.com/article/85413/10-historys-craziest-cat-people

Fear Free, LLC. (2018, February 6). Feline Intelligence: How Your Cat's Brain Works. Fear Free Happy Homes. https://www.fearfreehappyhomes.com/feline-intelligence-how-your-cats-brain-works/

Feathers & Fur Express. (2022, May 17). International Pet Shipping Costs. Feathers & Fur Express. https://ffexpresspets.com/international-pet-shipping-costs/

Four Paws International. (2021a, October 29). A Cat's Personality. FOUR PAWS International - Animal Welfare Organisation. https://www.four-paws.org/our-stories/publications-guides/a-cats-personality

Four Paws International. (2021b, October 29). Cats and Their Hunting Behaviour. FOUR PAWS International - Animal Welfare Organisation. https://www.four-paws.org/our-stories/publications-guides/cats-and-their-hunting-behaviour

Gelatt, K. N. (2018). Eye Structure and Function in Cats. Veterinary Manual; MSD Veterinary

Manual. https://www.msdvetmanual.com/cat-owners/eye-disorders-of-cats/eye-structure-and-function-in-cats

Gibson, Y. (2022, August 8). World Record Cats. Omlet Blog US. https://blog.omlet.us/2022/08/08/world-record-cats/

Golly Gear. (2022, January 22). The "Social Intelligence" of Dogs - GollyGear Blog about dogs. GollyGear Blog. https://www.gollygear.com/blog/2022/01/soc ial-intelligence-of-dogs/

Greenhalg, J. (2016, June 15). Cats understand the laws of physics and cause-and-effect. BBC Science Focus Magazine. https://www.sciencefocus.com/nature/cats-understand-the-laws-of-physics-and-cause-and-effect/

Gruner, J. A. (1989). Comparison of vestibular and auditory startle responses in the rat and cat. Journal of Neuroscience Methods, 27(1), 13–23. https://doi.org/10.1016/0165-0270(89)90049-6

Hale, T. (2023, February 17). Cat People Are More Intelligent, But Dog Lovers Have Their Positives Too. IFLScience. https://www.iflscience.com/cat-people-are-more-intelligent-but-dog-lovers-have-their-positives-too-67592

Holland, N. (2017, April 23). Tiger And Tom: The Cats Of The Bronte Sisters. Anne Brontë.

https://www.annebronte.org/2017/04/23/tige
r-and-tom-the-cats-of-the-bronte-sisters/

HuffPost Science. (2014, May 29). Cat People Are
Smarter Than Dog People, New Study Shows.
HuffPost.
https://www.huffpost.com/entry/cat-people-
dog-people-intelligence_n_5412245

Huggler, J. (2015, November 19). Neuter your cat or
put it on a leash, says German government.
Www.telegraph.co.uk.
https://www.telegraph.co.uk/news/worldnews
/europe/germany/12006529/Neuter-your-cat-
or-put-it-on-a-leash-says-German-
government.html

The Humane Society of the United States. (2023). Why
declawing is bad for your cat. The Humane
Society   of   the   United   States.
https://www.humanesociety.org/resources/wh
y-declawing-bad-your-cat

Hunter, T., & Buzhardt, L. (2023). Why Do Cats Have
Whiskers?   Vca_corporate.
https://vcahospitals.com/know-your-pet/why-
do-cats-have-whiskers

Infoplease. (2022). Household Pet Ownership, 1990–
2011.   Www.infoplease.com.
https://www.infoplease.com/us/family-
statistics/household-pet-ownership-1990-2013

Interzoo. (2021, April 15). The German pet market in
2020: More revenue, more pets | Interzoo.
Www.interzoo.com.
https://www.interzoo.com/en/news/newslette

r/2021-newsletter-april4-
ds0c8yucj4_pireport#:~:text=Cats%20are%20s
till%20the%20favourite

Jackson Galaxy Enterprises. (2017, November 9). Your
Cat's Behavior, Cat Mojo 101. Jackson Galaxy.
https://www.jacksongalaxy.com/blog/your-
cats-behavior-cat-mojo-101/

Jensen, L. (2015, June 26). 17 Basic Differences
Between Dog People And Cat People. Thought
Catalog; Thought Catalog.
https://thoughtcatalog.com/lorenzo-jensen-
iii/2015/06/17-basic-differences-between-dog-
people-and-cat-people/

Johnson-Bennett, P. (2012, May 14). What is the
Vomeronosal Organ in Cats?
Catbehaviorassociates.com.
https://catbehaviorassociates.com/what-is-the-
vomeronasal-organ/

Kelley, J. A. (2017, October 13). 8 Interesting Facts
About the Cat Nose and the Cat Sense of Smell.
Catster. https://www.catster.com/lifestyle/cat-
facts-cats-noses-sense-of-smell-pictures-photos

Kelley, T. L. (2022, April 13). Do Cats Love Their
Owners? Here's How to Tell. Daily Paws.
https://www.dailypaws.com/cats-
kittens/behavior/cat-psychology/do-cats-love-
their-owners

Kerr, K.-A. (2022, November 1). Is It True That All
Cats Have Henry's Pocket? What You Need to
Know! Excited Cats.

https://excitedcats.com/is-it-true-that-all-cats-have-henrys-pocket

King, B. J. (2017, February 16). Pet-Directed Speech May Convey Intentions In Subtle Ways. NPR.org. https://www.npr.org/sections/13.7/2017/02/16/515525984/using-pet-directed-speech-with-dogs-may-convey-intentions-in-subtle-ways

Ling, T. (2023, March 29). Why you're stroking your cat completely wrong (and how to do it right). BBC Science Focus Magazine. https://www.sciencefocus.com/nature/how-to-stroke-a-cat/

Mark, J. J. (2012, November 17). Cats in the Ancient World. World History Encyclopedia. https://www.worldhistory.org/article/466/cats-in-the-ancient-world/

McCarthy, E. (2019, July 10). 11 Facts About Hemingway's Cats. Www.mentalfloss.com. https://www.mentalfloss.com/article/587504/hemingways-cats-facts

Megna, M. (2023, April 10). Pet Ownership Statistics and Facts in 2023 – Forbes Advisor. Www.forbes.com. https://www.forbes.com/advisor/pet-insurance/pet-ownership-statistics

Miller, J. (2018, November 9). Bohemian Rhapsody: Freddie Mercury and His Cats, a Love Story. Vanity Fair Blogs. https://www.vanityfair.com/hollywood/2018/

11/freddie-mercury-and-his-love-affair-with-his-cats

Nastasi, A. (2018, September 13). 10 Famous Authors and Their Cats. PublishersWeekly.com. https://www.publishersweekly.com/pw/by-topic/industry-news/tip-sheet/article/77982-10-authors-and-their-cats.html

Natusan. (2023). PAWS FOR THOUGHT: 5 paw-some facts about cat's feet. Natusan. https://natusan.co.uk/blogs/inside-scoop/paws-for-thought

Newman, S. (2013, February 25). Cat Facts: Cat Hair 101. Fullyfeline.com. https://fullyfeline.com/cat-facts-cat-hair-101/

Noe, R. (2018, November 23). An Observant Mechanical Engineer's Discovery of Surprising Cat Tongue Properties. Core77. https://www.core77.com/posts/81178/An-Observant-Mechanical-Engineers-Discovery-of-Surprising-Cat-Tongue-Properties

Nolen, R. S. (2017, October 11). Study describes pet cat personality. American Veterinary Medical Association. https://www.avma.org/javma-news/2017-11-01/study-describes-pet-cat-personality

O'Brien, C. (2022, February 28). Cat Tongues: Everything You Wanted to Know & More | Hill's Pet. Hill's Pet Nutrition. https://www.hillspet.com/cat-care/behavior-appearance/cat-tongues-explained?lightboxfired=true#

Oster, L. (2022, February 11). A Colorful History of Cats in the White House. Smithsonian Magazine. https://www.smithsonianmag.com/history/a-colorful-history-of-cats-in-the-white-house-180979561/

Peters, S. (2017, December 11). See how far this Gardens Siamese cat leaps for Guinness World Record. The Palm Beach Post. https://www.palmbeachpost.com/story/news/local/2017/12/12/see-how-far-this-gardens/7023658007/

Pester, P. (2023, March 23). Legendary "cat-fox" could be a new subspecies. Livescience.com. https://www.livescience.com/legendary-cat-fox-could-be-a-new-subspecies

Pet Travel, Inc. (2023). Airline Pet Travel by Air - Pet Travel. Www.pettravel.com. https://www.pettravel.com/0001216.cfm

Pet-Express. (2019). How much does it cost to Fly a Cat Internationally? Pet Express. https://pet-express.com/blog/how-much-does-it-cost-to-fly-a-cat-internationally-pet-express/

Plotts, E. (2022, September 18). 5 Interesting Facts About Cat Teeth You Should Know. Pawlicy Advisor. https://www.pawlicy.com/blog/cat-teeth-facts/#issues

Price, C. (2023, June 6). Most Populous Animals On Earth. WorldAtlas. https://www.worldatlas.com/animals/most-populous-animals-on-earth.html

Prophet Muhammad PBUH Loved Cats and Muezza Was His Favorite Cat. (2020, May 13). https://theislamicinformation.com/blogs/prophet-muhammad-pbuh-muezza-favorite-cat/

Purina. (2022). Purring. Purina.com.au. https://www.purina.com.au/cats/behaviour/purring#:~:text=Purring%20involves%20the%20rapid%20movement

Purina. (2023). What Human Foods Can Cats Eat? | Purina. Www.purina.co.uk. https://www.purina.co.uk/articles/cats/feeding/what-cats-eat/human-foods-for-cats

The Purrfect Post. (2020). Healing Purrs: How Your Cat Can Help You Heal | PurrfectPost.com. Purrfectpost.com; PurrfectPost. https://www.purrfectpost.com/healing-purrs-how-your-cat-can-help-you-heal/

The Purring Journal. (2022, July 15). Top 10 Countries With the Most Pet Cats. The Purring Journal. https://thepurringjournal.com/blog/top-10-countries-with-the-most-pet-cats/

Purringtonpost. (2017, December 3). 9 Iconic Artists Who Loved Cats - The Purrington Post. Www.thepurringtonpost.com. https://www.thepurringtonpost.com/artists-and-cats/

Qureshi, A. I., Memon, M. Z., Vazquez, G., & Suri, M. F. K. (2009). Cat ownership and the Risk of Fatal Cardiovascular Diseases. Results from the Second National Health and Nutrition Examination Study Mortality Follow-up Study.

Journal of Vascular and Interventional Neurology, 2(1), 132–135. https://www.ncbi.nlm.nih.gov/pmc/articles/PMC3317329/

Randall, I. (2019, June 19). Mythical "cat-fox" that long evaded science may be new species. Mail Online. https://www.dailymail.co.uk/sciencetech/article-7157417/Mythical-cat-fox-Corsica-long-evaded-scientists-new-species.html

Richards, J. R. (2023). Cornell Center for Materials Research - Why are cats so flexible? Www.ccmr.cornell.edu. https://www.ccmr.cornell.edu/faqs/why-are-cats-so-flexible/

SANIBEL-CAPTIVA - Island Reporter, Islander and Current. (2020, April 7). Safe at Sea: Superstitions of sailors. Captivasanibel.com/. https://www.captivasanibel.com/2020/04/07/safe-at-sea-superstitions-of-sailors/

Schelling, C. (2022). Home - Declawing.com. Declawing.com. https://www.declawing.com/

Shiller, J. (2023). Florence Nightingale: Cats. Www.countryjoe.com. http://www.countryjoe.com/nightingale/cats.htm

Shojai, A. (2019). Is Your Cat Trying to Say They Love You? The Spruce Pets. https://www.thesprucepets.com/how-cats-show-love-553978

Shojai, A. (2022, March 21). Why Do Cats Show Their Butts? The Spruce Pets. https://www.thesprucepets.com/cat-butt-presentation-553910

Smith, A. (2017, June 21). Cats and Laser Pointers: Pros, Cons, and Safety Tips. Petfeed - Pet Care Tips, How-to Guides, Funny Stories, Comics, and Videos. https://petcube.com/blog/is-it-bad-for-cats-to-play-with-laser-pointers/

Sprabary, A. (2023). Cat Vision. All about Vision. https://www.allaboutvision.com/resources/human-interest/cat-vision

Stall, S. (2011). 100 Cats Who Changed Civilization. Quirk Books.

Starwood Pet Travel. (2019a, January 30). Cats and Crates: Tips for Comfortable Air Travel. Starwoodpet.com. https://starwoodpet.com/blog/cats-and-crates-tips-for-comfortable-air-travel

Starwood Pet Travel. (2019b, March 4). Should I Sedate My Cat for Overseas Travel? Starwoodpet.com. https://starwoodpet.com/blog/should-i-sedate-my-cat-for-overseas-travel

Starwood Pet Travel. (2019c, October 28). Airlines and Flat-Faced Dogs or Cats. Starwoodpet.com. https://starwoodpet.com/blog/airlines-and-flat-faced-dogs-or-cats

Syufy, F. (2019). Is There a Difference Between Cat Fur and Cat Hair? The Spruce Pets.

https://www.thesprucepets.com/cat-fur-vs-hair-554813

Tavernier, C., Ahmed, S., Houpt, K. A., & Yeon, S. C. (2020). Feline vocal communication. Journal of Veterinary Science, 21(1). https://doi.org/10.4142/jvs.2020.21.e18

Taylor, I. (2022, August 8). What Does It Mean When a Cat Kneads? The Spruce Pets. https://www.thesprucepets.com/why-do-cats-knead-5443073

Uys, C. (2022, December 7). Exploring the Cats of the Rich and Famous: 20 Celebrity Cats! Conscious Cat. https://consciouscat.net/exploring-the-cats-of-the-rich-and-famous/

Vocelle, L. A. (2014, February 28). Cats in the 19th Century (Part 5 – Famous Cat Lovers). THE GREAT CAT. https://www.thegreatcat.org/cats-19th-century-part-5-famous-cat-lovers/

Walkerville Vet. (2022). Do Cats Ever Smother Babies? Cat Dangers | Walkerville Vet. Www.walkervillevet.com.au. https://www.walkervillevet.com.au/blog/cats-smothering-babies/

Waynick, L. (2022, September 23). Why Does My Cat Follow Me Around Everywhere? The Spruce Pets. https://www.thesprucepets.com/why-does-my-cat-follow-me-everywhere-6455471

Weintraub, P. (2021, July 29). How Smart Is Your Cat? Here's How to Tell. Reader's Digest.

https://www.rd.com/list/how-smart-is-your-cat/

What's happening in your country? France | International Cat Care. (2020, September 29). Icatcare.org. https://icatcare.org/whats-happening-in-your-country-france/

Wu, K. (2021, December 27). 8 Reasons Your Cat Will Always Be Your "Baby" | Psychology Today. Www.psychologytoday.com. https://www.psychologytoday.com/intl/blog/the-modern-heart/202112/8-reasons-your-cat-will-always-be-your-baby

Yong, E. (2016, February 2). The Weird Thing About Cat Legs. The Atlantic. https://www.theatlantic.com/science/archive/2016/02/the-weird-thing-about-cat-legs/459369/

Made in the USA
Monee, IL
04 December 2023

48162556R00090